Transforming Faith

Stories of Change from a
Lifelong Spiritual Seeker

Fred Howard

ISBN: 1502521806
ISBN-13: 9781502521804
Library of Congress Control Number: 2014917503
CreateSpace Independent Publishing Platform
North Charleston, South Carolina

To Kathy,
Thanks for sharing the journey with me.

.

Contents

Preface vii
Introduction 1

Part I: Imagination **9**
Chapter 1: Difficult to Imagine 11
Chapter 2: But Just Imagine 16
Chapter 3: Confessions of a Failed Literalist. 22
Chapter 4: A Fish Out of Water. 27
Chapter 5: Lessons from a Toolshed 33
Chapter 6: The Holy Grail of Religious Authority 39

Part II: Faith **47**
Chapter 7: Questioning Faith. 49
Chapter 8: Transforming Faith 57
Chapter 9: Stages of Faith Development 65
Chapter 10: The Apostle Paul—Paradigm of Adopted Faith 75
Chapter 11: Bertrand Russell—Paradigm of Individuating Faith. . . 85
Chapter 12: Gandhi—Paradigm of Holistic Faith 93
Chapter 13: The Life Force Power of the Universe 102

Part III: Growth and Compassion **111**
Chapter 14: A Seminal Experience. 113
Chapter 15: Can We Talk?. 118

Chapter 16: Discerning the Call 125
Chapter 17: The Lost Art of Welcoming the Soul. 130
Chapter 18: The Canary in the Coal Mine 138

Part IV: God **145**
Chapter 19: God in the Third Dimension. 147
Chapter 20: What If God Was One of Us? 154
Chapter 21: God and Civility 160
Chapter 22: Meeting in Rumi's Field. 167

Part V: Christianity **175**
Chapter 23: Finding Spiritual Treasure 177
Chapter 24: Healing the Wounds of Our Religious Past 184
Chapter 25: What Kind of People Shall We Be?. 190
Chapter 26: Resurrecting the Resurrection. 197
Chapter 27: Why I Still Self-Identify as a Christian 204

Postscript. 213
Acknowledgments. 217
Selected Bibliography. 219
Endnotes 221
Author Biography 229

Preface

God made man because he loves stories.[A]
-Elie Wiesel

Stories shape our lives. Storytelling begins in childhood when our parents share their experiences to help us understand and cope with life's challenges. Once we are in school, our circle of learning grows ever larger. Our teachers tell stories as a way of getting us up to speed on the accumulated wisdom of humankind. When they teach us history, that's what their really doing – telling us the story of our past. Science and technology are stories also—stories concerning new ways to think about ourselves and the world around us. We learn best when someone imparts wisdom to us in the form of stories.

Whatever we retain of our early religious instruction also likely takes the form of stories. I have very few memories of the Sunday school teachers of my formative years, but I remember the biblical stories, and they continue to have a deep resonance within me. Today I might frame them as myth rather than actual occurrences. However, even now I can still recall those first images my childhood imagination created of events—Samson destroying the temple with his superhuman strength, Daniel surviving in the lion's den, and Jesus letting the little children come to him over his disciples' protests. No matter how much I learn about the Bible or how sophisticated my understanding of it becomes, I'll forever be shaped by the stories it contains and the way these stories were first introduced. Almost everything I've learned about the Divine has come to me in the form of stories.

Stories form our identities. It's difficult (if not impossible) to understand ourselves unless we have stories to tell ourselves about who we are and who we are attempting to be in the world around us. If I call myself a minister, how do I understand that role? Do I seek to always be compassionate, or am I more interested in whatever self-aggrandizement might come as I perform the function of a minister? Whatever names you call yourself in life—parent, citizen, businessperson, or friend—the stories you tell yourself guide you along the way.

Having some idealized definition of what makes you a good parent or a good friend is well and good, but who wants to merely be the embodiment of a definition? The shaping of your core identity can't just be an intellectual enterprise. True identity arises in the heart and soul. These parts of ourselves go much deeper than the intellect, and they much prefer the playground of the imagination. As the mystery of you makes itself manifest in the world, little about who you are can be explained, but something of your essence can be captured when someone tells a story about you.

Theologian Harvey Cox says in the autobiographical account of his religious pilgrimage, *The Seduction of the Spirit,* "All human beings have an innate need to tell and hear stories and to have a story to live by. Religion, whatever else it has done, has provided one of the main ways of meeting this abiding need."[B] Stories that emerge as others tell me about their spiritual journeys have always held a particular fascination for me. Perhaps I'm so enchanted by such stories because of the poignancy of similar tales from my own odyssey. Such as the time when I felt such a comforting divine presence during a silent Christmas Eve communion service at a time of intense personal crisis. That I could experience something so powerful and real without a word being spoken irrevocably changed me in some small but significant way. In the wake of this event, even though I couldn't name the change, it became easier for me to be with others who were going through difficult times and I felt more genuine compassion for them. Another personal instance occurred when I was on a pilgrimage to Transylvania. My encounter with the people there who were such kindred spirits opened me up in so many ways. These people had little in the way of material possessions but had such a deep appreciation of family and community. One of my fellow pilgrims said it well, "These people are so poor, but they are so rich." Once I returned home, I had some difficulty reengaging with my former life, since I now looked at material possessions quite differently. Though its been quite a few years since that pilgrimage, much of that change in perspective stayed with me. And I'm so grateful for this gift given to me by those people in Transylvania.

For those of us in religious community, so much of who we are is shaped by our encounters there. In religious community we hear stories, and it is in the hearing and telling of these stories that I experience what I call God. It might seem a strange thing to say, but the only God I know personally is the one I see in others as we share stories and build community together.

My personal theology does not focus on belief but on what beliefs make of us. Individual beliefs are too often used to pigeonhole people and attach religious labels to them. While I might call myself a Unitarian or a Universalist, this term doesn't so much name a set of personal beliefs as it simply identifies a community with which I have chosen to associate. While I claim this identity, my ultimate goal is to be secure enough in that identity to venture forth, learn about the religions and cultures of others, and never be threatened by them.

As a physician I was intrigued when I learned the word "curiosity" shares the same linguistic root as "cure." When I am curious about other people and their experiences in the spiritual dimension, it sometimes feels as if I am entering some place of great destiny. When I and others are courageous enough to disclose bits of our spirits to each other, I have experienced this dimension as a place of great healing. When I listen to someone from a very different background who relates to the spiritual life in new, fascinating ways, I have the chance to gain a whole new perspective on the faith journey. Encounters such as these have expanding benefits for my spirit as well.

From very early on, I had an intellectual and emotional interest in other religions, and the myriad ways the divine manifests itself in the lives of people throughout the world continually fascinates me. That doesn't mean I find my own faith unsatisfactory. It simply means it's still incomplete. As I hear the stories of others' spiritual journeys, it's as if I'm able to fill in a few more pieces of a grand puzzle. Therefore, I remain open in a way that allows me to maintain my identity even as I continue to grow and develop through exposure to and challenge from the many sectors of religious experience.

It's important for us to continue telling the emotionally significant stories of our lives. Storytelling gives meaning and texture to existence. Strands of individual stories are woven together to create the social fabric in which we live and move and have our being.

We remember best through stories. Re-member. When we re-member, we are calling forth the memories that bind us together. Recalling and telling stories is how we claim membership in our families and communities. It's in the sharing of stories that we gain our sense of belonging.

What follows is my fledgling attempt toward that goal. In sharing my journey, I'll touch on several theological issues. I write as a minister, though, and not a theologian. I have no credentials other than my experience as a keen observer of how ideas about faith have acted in my life and in the lives of my parishioners. Not being a professional theologian has actually been advantageous as I worked out these ideas about religious faith. It allowed me to come at the subject fresh, with what Buddhists refer to as "beginner's mind." Instead of building on Emerson's "sepulchers of the fathers," I have endeavored to make faith more personal, relevant, and accessible to the twenty-first-century layperson. I hope my efforts prove useful to you on your spiritual journey.

* * *

Introduction

In the infancy of my spiritual life, I became part of a group of born-again Christians. This occurred at the impressionable age of eighteen during my freshman year in college. Being at college was my first time living away from home. That, combined with my natural introversion, made it a rather lonely time. I was set up for some group to come along looking for converts. This group offered friendship and acceptance, and the price of admission - accepting Jesus as my Lord and Savior – didn't seem like too high a price to pay. I'd been raised in the church and always thought Jesus was pretty cool, so it didn't bother me too much to go along with the rigid way they framed salvation. At first. For a few months, it felt pretty good to be inside a bounded community—a group of people who held the same religious ideals and were united around a common goal. That goal was to convince others to be saved and join the ranks of the true believers.

Most of this group's efforts to gain adherents were pretty inoffensive and noninvasive -gestures such as inviting others to come to church. However, they would occasionally get "into the Spirit" (to borrow a favorite phrase of theirs) and whip each other into a zealous frenzy. The group would then want to walk around campus, pass out tracts, and attempt to convert perfect strangers. "Witnessing" was what they called it. Perhaps a more correct term was "proselytizing."

Though I was pretty comfortable being a part of this group, I wasn't particularly comfortable with proselytizing. Something in me protested when I was asked to join in. This was where I was going to draw the line. At first my excuse was just my introverted nature. I didn't want to walk up to strangers and strike up conversations. Really, though, I didn't want to look like some sort of fanatic.

However, as I began to think further about what this group was doing and asking me to do, "witnessing" struck me as contrary to the most basic thing Jesus taught—the Golden Rule. As Jesus taught it, the Golden Rule says, "Do unto others as you would have them do unto you."[1] Since I didn't particularly like the idea of proselytizing in the first place, and I didn't want someone coming to try to convert me, then for me to do so to others, would be a direct violation of the Golden Rule. Simple enough. Right?

Of course it was not that simple. My friends in this Christian group had a ready answer for that one. When I explained my reason for not wanting to witness, they were horrified. They asked me, "If you realized you were in a burning building, wouldn't you want to tell others the building was on fire? That's what you're doing when you witness to others. You're saving them from burning in hell. You don't want to burn up in the building, and you would want others to tell you if the building is on fire. According to the Golden Rule, you're obligated to tell them about Jesus and that believing in him can save them from the fires of hell just as it saved you."

It was beginning to dawn on me that trying to reason with someone of a fundamentalist bent is pretty much a futile exercise. Bear with me, though. Persisting in my efforts actually turned out to be a worthwhile exercise. I never changed their minds, but I certainly developed confidence and conviction in my own thoughts and processing of the matter.

---

1 Matt. 7:12. New Revised Standard Version.

The impulse to convert others to your way of thinking is one of the strongest and most pervasive tendencies of the human religious experience. It's a nearly universal aspect of human nature to say, "If only they could be like me, the world would be a better place." When you combine that psychological tendency with the explicit declarations of religious founders to make converts of others, it's no wonder many members of the world's largest religions are out there trying to make converts. The Gospel of Matthew records Jesus as saying, "Go therefore and make disciples of all nations."[2] According to the Koran, Mohammed wrote, "We have sent you only as a bearer of good tidings and admonisher for all mankind."[3] According to the Buddhist tradition, Siddhartha Gautama told his followers, "Go forth, o monks, for the good of the many, for the happiness of the many, out of compassion for the world, for the good, benefit, and happiness of people...Teach the dharma, excellent in the beginning, excellent in the middle, and excellent in the end."[c] Followers of Christianity, Islam, and Buddhism can find ample justification for overt efforts to convert others to their religious traditions. This impetus toward conversion gains more and more momentum as people come together in groups, form communities for support and encouragement, establish norms for those communities, and then seek to spread and perpetuate these norms.

Many other reasons exist for our inclination toward converting others. If someone else holds a different opinion, it automatically leads us to question our own. Most people have trouble holding onto and giving credence to two seemingly contradictory ideas. Two contradictory ideas both containing the truth seems inconsistent to the rational mind. This inconsistency often causes a mental and psychological discomfort known as cognitive dissonance. The

---

2 Matt. 28:19.

3 Koran 34:28.

more important the belief, the more discomfort this dissonance creates. The more discomfort it causes, the more effort a person will make to resolve the inconsistency. There are two obvious ways an inconsistency between your beliefs and mine can be resolved. Either you change your mind and accept my belief as the truth, or I do the hard work of reimagining my beliefs and way of thinking and processing to be consistent with yours. Which of these usually wins out? The easier route, of course. The path of least resistance. Therefore, it's your belief that is in need of change.

Besides these reasons for our tendency toward proselytizing and conversion of others, there is yet one more payoff. If I can convince you to accept my belief as the path to truth and righteousness, then that makes me into something of a savior figure. For most of us, that's a real rush. If my belief wins out, then I get all kinds of psychological perks. However, if I allow you to persuade me, then there's very little in it for me. Yes. I might draw a little closer to the truth. But it might require me to reevaluate my whole system of belief, and that just takes too much thought and effort.

Let's go back to the Golden Rule. I don't want someone introducing me to a new belief or a new religion and calling my entire belief system into question. Since I don't want others to do that unto me, it would follow from the Golden Rule that I shouldn't do that unto others. Therefore, attempting to convert others to my religious beliefs would seem in direct violation of the Golden Rule.

Perhaps the Golden Rule is just not what it's cracked up to be. The Golden Rule, as good as it is in defining what it means to live an upright and moral life, is not immune to criticism. George Bernard Shaw put forth perhaps the most famous criticism. He quipped, "Do not do unto others as you would have them do unto you. Their tastes may not be the same." Shaw's point is well taken. The example of my overzealous friend from college years who felt compelled to proselytize others to save them from the fires of hell illustrates Shaw's point well. Our tastes are not the same, nor are our values, principles, and desires. If what you value and want from others is markedly different than what they value and want from you, then the way you want to be treated will not be the way they want to be treated. That is to say, treating others as you want to be treated is not automatically the key to transforming society into the kingdom of heaven. Others after Shaw issued a corrective to the Golden rule based on Shaw's sentiment. "Do unto others as they would have you do unto them." This has become known as the Platinum Rule.

There are problems, however, with the Platinum Rule as well. It's generally not in the best interest of a child or an immature adult to do unto him or her exactly as he or she wants. Children don't always know what's best for them. A child might want to eat eight chocolate bars at a time, for instance. The alcoholic on the street corner might want you to give him or her money to buy more alcohol. This would certainly not be in his or her best interest. Whether the Golden Rule, the Platinum Rule, or some other guideline directs your behavior, for an ethics of reciprocity to be truly ethical, some reflection must be done on what is ultimately in the best interest of the other.

Despite George Bernard Shaw's protest, the Golden Rule can still function as a gold standard for morality. However, we must be thoughtful and reflective about how we apply it. When we consider how to treat others based on how we want to be treated, we have to think beyond any specific act. You must consider the significance of that act for you and whether it would have the same significance for the other person. To do that well, you have to know the other person and be willing to treat him or her with the same respect you have for yourself. For example, consider gift giving. A couple love each other very much. He is more interested in giving and receiving verbal affirmation and nurture and has no interest in material things. She's not very verbal but loves and appreciates material tokens. Every time Valentine's Day, Christmas, or some other special occasion rolls around their relationship is inevitably stressed. During these times, he always remembers to be extra attentive and heaps on the praise and affection but sometimes "forgets" to pick up a gift. In contrast she spends endless hours fretting over purchasing just the right gift for him to the point that she's not home as much, and not as present to him even when she is around. He gives her compliments and she gives him stuff. They're both giving as they would like to receive. But both of them are unhappy and they can't figure out why. For the golden rule to work as it should, we must listen attentively and respond appropriately to the other based on a firm understanding of the other person.

It requires what Martin Buber called an I–Thou relationship. That is, you recognize the other person as separate and different from yourself but worthy of your honor and respect. The other person is a "thou"—a manifestation of the divine. If you fail to recognize the "thou" in the other person, you are in danger of developing what Buber called an I–It relationship. You will view that person merely as an object to be used in the advancement of your own goals and agenda. An I–It relationship is, at its core, a manifestation of narcissism. Just like the mythic figure Narcissus, who became so transfixed with his own image that everyone became for him a reflection of himself, so it is with people who are only capable of I–It relationships. They project their own needs onto other people and see them as objects in service to their own fulfillment.[D]

I would submit there is an element of narcissism in people trying to religiously proselytize. In my encounters with people caught up in such efforts, trying to have conversations with them is like talking to people who see everyone else as reflections of themselves. It often seems they are incapable of comprehending that others could have different needs, values, and viewpoints. For them there is no "other." There is only themselves and their fixed perceptions of the way to gain salvation.

The Golden Rule has served the world pretty well as the groundwork for a standard behavioral ethic. However, for that rule to work, there must be recognition of the otherness of fellow human beings. For people such as my zealous college friends, there didn't seem to be other beliefs and opinions deserving of recognition and respect. It's difficult for someone to follow the Golden Rule when others (or their values) don't even exist.

It makes for a relatively uncomplicated existence when all questions have pat answers and everything is seen in black and white. There is no need to expend any mental or emotional energy to make room for others' thoughts and reflections. But, my, how lonely it must be to construct such a world view for oneself where there is no other.

The Golden Rule can function well as the basis of a universal moral ethic so long as there is recognition of the otherness of others. Other people have unique needs, desires, perspectives, and interpretations of words and actions. Their tastes are not your tastes. For the Golden Rule to work as intended, we must be thoughtful about its application, as we would have others be thoughtful in applying it to us. If you simply assume others have the same needs and desires as you, then you are in danger of doing the same thing Narcissus did when he looked down in the pool and saw nothing but his own reflection. The reciprocity inherent in the Golden Rule means others are not projections of you. They are your neighbors. They are "thous." They are manifestations of the divine just as you are.

One way of understanding life is to see it as a journey. Others hold up mirrors to us and help us learn the myriad ways we consciously or subconsciously violate the Golden Rule almost every day of our lives. Only as we become more conscious of this do we start to more fully recognize the divine in others.

* * *

Part I

Imagination

one

Difficult to Imagine

My favorite uncle when I was growing up was Uncle Howard. He could have the first name Howard because he was on my mother's side of the family. Uncle Howard was very passionate about one particular hobby—rebuilding old cars. He had a tin-covered garage in his backyard, and it was the gathering place for all the men in his neighborhood. There was a makeshift stove where he and his buddies would make coffee and while away their leisure hours talking about cars or reminiscing about their days serving in the armed forces during World War II.

His favorite project was a salvaged Model T that took up permanent residence in one section of his garage. Rebuilding it became my uncle's lifelong project. I even remember riding around his old neighborhood in that Model T on a couple very rare occasions when he had reassembled enough of this old flivver so that it would actually run.

I remember well when Uncle Howard died. He was not a religious man by any stretch of the imagination. I doubt if he ever darkened the door of a church except on his wedding day and when he attended the occasional funeral. He was, however, in church on a particular day back in 1987. He was attending the one funeral every person attends—his or her own. He was in his casket and positioned in front of the church immediately below the pulpit. That was many years ago, and I doubt I would remember that funeral at all, but the preacher said one particular thing that really made the occasion come alive for me. He said, "I can see Brother Howard looking at us now from under the hood of that old Model T, and I can hear that big hearty laugh of his in that backyard garage up there in heaven."

That one statement came somewhere in the middle of what was otherwise a rather dry, colorless funeral service, and it made the entire occasion. In that moment it became a memorial service—a joyful remembering of my uncle's spirit. In that moment everyone in the church started laughing and began looking around at each other. They nodded in agreement that what the preacher had just said completely captured and encapsulated my uncle. It rang so true. We all saw him bent over the Model T. We smelled that odd combination of motor oil and coffee that always lingered near him, and we heard that gregarious laugh of his. We had an encounter with his spirit, and it was unbelievably real. The reality of that moment has stayed with me and has helped me keep the memories of my uncle alive.

However comforting this idea of my uncle looking down at us and sharing a laugh was and is, especially for his wife and children, it is not a part of Christian doctrine or theology.

In Christian doctrine the dead are dead in body and spirit and will remain so until the Day of Judgment. There is no such thing as a disembodied spirit who is already in heaven or free to walk the Earth to either haunt us or offer comfort. This idea that our loved ones are looking down on us from heaven (or the corner of the room) and offering comfort or occasional bits of encouragement and wisdom is inconsistent with what is largely taught in Christian churches. I'm not just referring to Christian churches of a fundamental or literalist stripe. Belief in an immortal soul or spirit that survives bodily death is neither a part of the findings of modern critical biblical scholarship nor its teachings. The biblical view is not that the human body has a soul. It is a soul. So when the body dies, so does the soul. That's why the creeds contain so much about the resurrection of the body. In the Christian view, God will one day resurrect body *and* spirit—face, voice, and peculiarities of temperament and talent - all the things that go into making each person a unique human being.

The idea of an immortal soul that goes on after physical death actually comes from paganism. Evidence suggests the concept was present in numerous preclassic folk and tribal religions, but it was Plato who popularized the idea in his writings during the classical Greek period.

When we hear people in churches speak about the dearly departed being in the "bosom of Abraham" or looking down on us from heaven, we are actually hearing a remnant of these pagan theologies. It is so powerful and comforting that it breaks through Christianity's formal, institutional theology.

I use the word "remnant" because in the early part of the first millennium, Christianity spread rapidly across Europe, and there were many attempts to exterminate the beliefs of the indigenous people. These attempts only accelerated as the Roman Empire spread and Christianity became the official religion of the Roman Empire. However, missionaries gradually learned that attempts to exterminate the beliefs of the native people were generally not successful. The mythology and symbolism of those native religions was simply too strong and too basic to the human psyche to be obliterated. So missionaries developed a strategy. Rather than try to exterminate native people's customs and beliefs, the pope instructed his missionaries to use them. If a group of people worshipped a tree, rather than cut it down, the pope advised the missionaries to consecrate it to Christ and allow its continued worship.

When St. Patrick and other Christian missionaries went to Ireland, many of the existing pagan practices became incorporated into Christian feast days and festivals. Pope Boniface IV decided to designate November 1 All Saints' Day—a time to honor saints and martyrs. It is widely believed today the pope was attempting to replace the Celtic festival of the dead with a related but church-sanctioned holiday.

In terms of spreading Christianity, this was a brilliant concept, and it became a basic approach used in Catholic missionary work. The church's holy days were purposely set to coincide with native holy days.

All Saints' Day, otherwise known as All Hallows, continued the ancient Celtic traditions. "Hallowed" actually means sanctified or holy. In Celtic practice the evening prior to the festival of the dead was the time of the most intense human and supernatural activity. After Christianity arrived, people continued to celebrate All Hallows' Eve as a time of the wandering dead, but the supernatural beings were now thought evil. The people continued to propitiate those spirits (and their masked impersonators) by setting out gifts of food and drink. Subsequently All Hallows' Eve became Hallow Evening, and that became Hallowe'en—an ancient Celtic, pre-Christian New Year's Day – now in contemporary dress.

Many ancient Celtic customs such as the festival of the dead just described (also known as Samhain) proved compatible with the new Christian religion. Christianity embraced the Celtic notions of family, community, the bond among all people, and respect for the dead. Therefore many ancient traditions, such as Samhain, never died out. However Christianity managed to affect major transformations in it. The Celtic gods became transmuted into demonic figures, and the Celtic underworld inevitably became identified with the Christian hell. Followers who persisted in practicing the old religion were branded devil worshippers or witches and forced to go into hiding.[E]

It might seem odd to make a festive occasion out of a day associated with dead people's spirits returning to visit, but the same phenomenon occurs in Latin America with the *Día de Los Muertos*, the Day of the Dead. This is also celebrated at this time of year. Altars are made to commemorate departed loved ones with pictures and other remembrances, and the family shares in the favorite foods and beverages of the deceased. There are sugar skulls for the kids and dancing skeletons in the streets. Through all this the sting of death is lessened and the prospect of going on without the lost ones is not so difficult to bear.

That such rituals have sprung up independently in various cultures around the world bears witness to an intense need in the human psyche and spirit to touch and be touched by our loved ones who are no longer among us physically. In a fundamental sense, it's the same need that stirred me and the others at my uncle's funeral many years ago. There is something very basic in humans that needs this way of conceptualizing the spirit world. I need this idea of an immortal soul that might stay in this plane of existence for a time or soon move to a better place. I am grateful for this way of imaging what comes next for me and my loved ones—whatever its source.

We need to use our imaginations to engage with unseen things. There's something about the thoughts and images of a spirit world that we go to when we depart that is of inestimable value when dealing with grief and getting through this terminal condition of being human. Being dead, body and soul, until Judgment Day just doesn't do it for me. I don't think I'm alone in this. I don't know where that pigeonholes me in terms of religion. I don't really care. I just know it works for me in my faith journey.

* * *

two

But Just Imagine

"Reality leaves a lot to the imagination."
—John Lennon

"Imagine"

Imagine there's no heaven.
It's easy if you try.
No hell below us,
Above us only sky.
Imagine all the people
Living for today...

Imagine there's no countries.
It isn't hard to do.
Nothing to kill or die for
And no religion too.
Imagine all the people
Living life in peace...

You may say I'm a dreamer,
But I'm not the only one.
I hope someday you'll join us,
And the world will be as one.

Imagine no possessions.
I wonder if you can.
No need for greed or hunger,
A brotherhood of man.
Imagine all the people
Sharing all the world...

You may say I'm a dreamer,
But I'm not the only one.
I hope someday you'll join us,
And the world will live as one.[F]

Imagine how surprised John Lennon must have been at the wild popularity of this little ditty he wrote. Sitting at an upright Steinway piano in his bedroom in 1971, he composed the melody, chord structure, and almost all the lyrics in one brief session. Released later that same year, the song climbed as high as number three on America's *Billboard* top one hundred, and the LP of the same name reached number one in the United Kingdom. To date the single has sold more than 1.6 million copies in the United Kingdom alone. *Rolling Stone* magazine ranked it as the third greatest song of all time. Not bad for a single morning's work.

People have come up with a lot of theories to explain why such a simple song is so wildly popular and stirs us on such a deep level. I have a theory as well. I've done a lot of Google searches on this theory, and as far as I can tell, no one else has thought of it. A unique idea. Imagine that?

To explain I need to elaborate a little bit about imagination. Imagination is the capacity to picture things that might or might not exist in the material world. Imagination allows us to create inner worlds, and each of our inner worlds is a unique dimension of human experience. Imagination is also an essential part of the capacity to learn. Twenty-six phonetic symbols, ten numerals, and a few punctuation marks can represent every word ever written or spoken since the dawn of time. Imagination takes in these symbols and translates them into mental images. They go from scribbles on a page into our private re-creations of the past or future. We read the words of the Aeneid and imagine Odysseus defeating the Trojans with a wooden horse or Martians invading Earth in a sci-fi tale.

Since we learn and create our inner lives with imagination, this capacity also makes us religious or spiritual beings. Scripture, symbols, metaphors, and rituals have no meaning unless imagination translates them into emotionally resonant images and stories that make those deep connections to the spirit. God, for instance, is something that can't be seen, heard, felt, or touched in any material or physical sense. The word "God," like every other religious word, has connotations. It brings up experiential memories, and we make associations between these things. We then construct meaning around the word. All these mental processes involve imagination.

Even a spirituality that doesn't require a god still requires imagination. How so? All the world's major religious and spiritual traditions have some version of the Golden Rule as the basis for their morality. In order to love your neighbor as you do yourself, you must use imagination to approximate what that neighbor's life is like. Through imagination you must walk a mile in his or her shoes.

Great religious teachers throughout the ages have recognized the power and potential of the human imagination. That's why so many of them taught by using stories. Nothing else captures the imagination quite like a story. Storytelling is and has always been humanity's fundamental way of communicating. No other way of conveying information works quite as effectively. Stories make information interesting, memorable, and even persuasive. Jesus and the Buddha knew this. That's why they taught using parables. Jesus is even said to have taught exclusively in stories. The gospel writer Mark said, "He did not speak to them except in parables."[4]

A rabbi was once asked, "Why does the parable possess such great influence?"

The wise rabbi replied, "I will explain this with a parable.

"Truth was accustomed to walking about as naked as he was born. No one allowed him to enter a home, and everyone who encountered him ran away in fright. Truth felt greatly embittered and could find no resting place. One day he beheld Parable attired in colorful, expensive garments. Parable inquired, 'Why are you so dejected, my friend?' Truth replied, 'I am in a bad situation. I am very old, and no one cares to have anything to do with me.' 'Nay,' retorted Parable. 'It is not because of your age people dislike you. Look. I am as old as you are, and the older I grow, the more do I seem to be loved. Let me disclose to you the secret of my apparent popularity. People enjoy seeing everything dressed up and somewhat disguised. Let me lend you my garments, and you will see that people will like you as well.'

"Truth followed this counsel and dressed himself in Parable's garments. Ever since then, Truth and Parable walk hand in hand, and people love them both."[G]

It seems the capacity to imagine is essential to religion. It might be a rather dangerous thing to say, but on some level human beings imagined religions into existence. Without imagination religion (as a human phenomenon) could not even exist.

When I speak of imagination in religion and spirituality, I'm not referring to imagination as "making stuff up." I'm definitely not

<hr>

4 Mark 4:34.

trying to belittle imagination or religion. I'm saying that religion is imaginative. Not imaginary. When the word "imaginary" is used, it's usually meant to disparage. As one comedian said, "Religion. Who needs it? People fussing and fighting. Even going to war for the sake of their religion. People actually do that. Kill each other over who has the best imaginary friend."[5]

On the contrary the capacity to imagine might be a human being's finest quality. It's what puts us on the royal road to our deeper consciousness and our creativity. It allows us to transcend the mean, indifferent constraints of present reality. It's what empowers us to envision a better world.

So when John Lennon sings, "Imagine there's no heaven and no religion too," it suddenly hits us like a full body slam. Why would we need to use our imaginations to envision a world without religion when religion would not exist for us in the first place if we had not imagined it into being at some earlier point in life? The lyrics themselves are straightforward, and there's not a bit of irony in them. However, anyone who gives them more than a passing thought is confronted with the irony of ironies. We have a world full of religions and various notions of heaven. All are supposedly meant to bring about human fulfillment, joy, and peace. Yet the path to peace just might lie in the opposite direction.

This irony has obviously hit home with many people through the years. The truth in this irony suggests we consider the obvious. The world has tried religion, and it just isn't working. Rather than fostering world peace, religions continue to give nearly daily justification for violence and war.

Is it any wonder that Lennon's song finds resonance in the human heart? Wouldn't envisioning the world Lennon suggests be a better use of human imagination? Is his utopian vision any more

---

5 Many comedians have said similar things. It's unclear with whom this originated.

absurd than continuing to live the way we're living when what we're doing obviously isn't making the world a more peaceful place?

In a 1980 interview, Lennon said, "If you can *imagine* a world at peace, with no denominations of religion—not without religion but without this my-God-is-bigger-than-your-God thing—then it can be true...[T]he World Church called me once and asked, 'Can we use the lyrics to "Imagine" and just change it to "Imagine *one* religion"?' That showed they didn't understand it at all. It would defeat the whole purpose of the song, the whole idea."[H]

The song works because it does not preach. It merely invites. It's a protest song, and yet it's not mired in anger or blame. It calmly and patiently submits its alternative of hope and inclusivity. Its simple, almost melancholy melody is written in the feel-good key of C major—a rather odd choice for a protest song. However, in such contrasts, musical genius sometimes manifests itself and destines a song to become a classic.

The song invites us to imagine living life without the idea of an afterlife (i.e., neither a heaven nor a hell as reward or punishment). "Above us only sky." This might just get us to focus on salvation in this life and work to make this a better world in the here and now.

Our imagination frees us from the constraints of the world as it is, and we can dream dreams about the world as it might be. Imagine the difference you can make in another person's life just by being his or her friend or by being a part of a community where everyone is welcomed and allowed to express himself or herself without fear of judgment or being spiritually abused. Imagine. It's not so hard to do.

> "You may say I'm a dreamer,
> But I'm not the only one.
> I hope someday you'll join us,
> And the world will live as one."

* * *

three

Confessions of a Failed Literalist

"I have a story that will make you believe in God."[1] One of the characters at the beginning of *Life of Pi* states this claim. The novel is a coming-of-age story about a pious young man from India who makes a most improbable trip across the Pacific Ocean in a lifeboat with a whole menagerie of zoo animals. This includes a Bengal tiger. To read the book is to place yourself at the mercy of a great storyteller named Yann Martel. Martel makes this fantastical tale perfectly believable through his meticulous attention to detail and descriptions so vivid the reader can actually taste the salty air, feel the sun mercilessly baking Pi's skin for days on end, and see the boundless horizon of water one would expect to encounter in the middle of the Pacific. Pi's life is stripped of all nonessentials during his 227-day voyage, and he survives by throwing himself into the practical details of catching fish, collecting rainwater, protecting himself from the sun, and training the Bengal tiger—the only other survivor of the journey once the tiger has consumed all the other animals. Pi eventually makes it through the near starvation and constant danger from sharks and the ever-menacing tiger through his consummate use of logic and tenacious will to live.[J]

When he finally arrives in Mexico, company officials of the doomed ship question him extensively. These officials are only interested in facts—to ascertain blame for the sinking of the ship and to settle insurance claims. Despite his best efforts to convince them of the truth of his incredible tale, they do not believe him. So Pi ends up telling them a second version of the story with no animals and only other humans. It is a much more gruesome but believable story. When Pi discovers they believe the second story but not the first (without proof to substantiate either), he asks his inquisitors, "Since it makes no factual difference to you, and you can't prove the question either way, which story do you prefer? Which is the better story—the story with animals or the story without animals?" The officials agree the story with animals is the better story. Pi replies to them, "Thank you. And so it goes with God."[K]

And so it goes with God. Martel's point seems to be that the idea of "God" makes for the better story. This novel has enjoyed tremendous success since its publication in 2001 and has gained quite a cult following. Martel has been questioned extensively about his mind-set in writing the novel, especially in regard to its religious overtones. In an interview not long after the book's publication, he said, "The theme of the novel can be summarized in three sentences. Life is a story. You can choose your story. And a story with an imaginative overlay is the better story." Martel went on to say the greatest imaginative overlay is religion. "God," according to Martel, "is a shorthand for anything that is beyond the material—any greater pattern of meaning."[L]

Martel took on the challenge of writing *Life of Pi* as an effort to overcome his cynicism in regard to religion. As he began to research and write, he began to find value in religious faith. In crafting the novel, Martel used the name Pi for the story's protagonist. Pi is a mathematical symbol, but it also has wonderful parallels to the religious quest. Martel said, "Pi is one of those basic numbers that is used in science to explore the world. It's used constantly in engineering, in mathematics. Yet it's an irrational number. To me, religion is like that. It's irrational, but it makes sense of the universe."[M]

In my religious journey, there was a time when I bought into the concept of God as a literal, factual reality. Over time I have moved away from that way of trying to come to grips with the great mystery we are all participating in. I am still comfortable with the notion of something (a cosmic force of some sort) that somehow set up life the way it is. Call it God. Call it...whatever. Whether God exists or not in a literal sense is no longer relevant to my faith. For me "God" is better understood as a convention of speech. God is a common way for people to speak of ultimate things and the deeper meanings in life. Having adopted this understanding, it's easier for me to hear others when they use God language. Now I no longer get distracted from listening because I might disagree with them over whether or not God "exists." Because even if their understanding is more literal, that's okay. Literal God or not, it's still their way of attempting to communicate ultimate meaning.

German philosopher Ludwig Feuerbach said it better than I ever could. "People create gods to express the spiritual significance of life, just as the artist creates a work of art in order to express his or her awareness of beauty."[N] What a beautiful way to express the existential dilemma. As a statement in poetic prose, I agree with Feuerbach. Does that make me a theist or an atheist? The question would seem to have no relevance in this context.

I use the word "God" to express myself, but I do so sparingly. To speak of God risks being understood as speaking of or even for an active, creative entity within or behind the universe. This entity sometimes takes sides, sometimes heals, and sometimes doesn't. The use of God language often seems a little presumptuous to me, and so I hesitate. Part of this reservation also stems from the atrocious projections I have heard other people make when speaking of or to God. However, I do listen when people speak of God whether or not they say they are believers. This is, after all, one of the ways people tell their stories. I learn a lot about them from what they say about God, but I don't know if I necessarily learn much about God.

As for the idea of a personal God, the only God I know personally is the divine I find in others. In my role as a chaplain at Emory Hospital, I was privileged to be at the bedside of several patients near death. Many of them still lucid and strong enough to talk wanted to tell me their stories. I heard from people who believed in God, and I heard from a few who didn't. Almost every person used the word "God" at some point in the conversation, even if used to negate the idea. Each person used the term as a way of describing his or her relationship to the universe and to everything that held ultimate meaning for that person. Even if the testimony was a negation of the idea of a creator God, I felt I was in the presence of divinity because of the poignancy of the situation and the power of the story shared about what gave richness and depth to his or her life.

To really hear the other person's story I found I had to suspend any disbelief I might have about his or her deity. It was just how I had to suspend disbelief when I went to the movies. Doing ministry is a lot like going to the movies. I must get caught up in the story the person is telling, and to do that I must find a little of myself in that person and his or her story. Just like when I go to the movies, I must find something of myself in one of the characters. Deep listening (like moviegoing) is an act of faith. The person or story unfolding before me needs to become believable. The question of whether or not I agree intellectually is irrelevant to the greater purpose for which I am there.

Yann Martel said in another interview about *Life of Pi* that most people who had been teased into reading the book by that audacious claim (that it was a story that would make them believe in God) looked for proof of God in the story. These people came away disappointed. The people who found God because there was a story—a magnificent story of tenacity and faith—were the ones who got what Martel was saying. He was not out to prove the existence of God but to prove that a belief in God is justifiable. I am in the same boat with Pi (if you will forgive the awful pun) because God is the better story for me. I find the idea of God necessary to express the spiritual significance of my life.

* * *

four

A Fish Out of Water

I have many fond memories of my years in the Baptist church—
church suppers, Sunday school socials, retreats at Camp Ridgecrest
in North Carolina, and church league softball games. I spent nearly
twenty years of my life in that religious tradition, so I was bound to
make a lot of friends and develop a sense of community within the
congregations of which I became a part. I've never felt more of a
sense of community than I experienced within that faith tradition.
After all, I was a part of a group where most everyone held similar
beliefs. It was relatively easy to fit in. I got quite comfortable in a
place where I expected people to think and behave in predictable
ways.

The Baptist church is also where I "got saved." In revivalist traditions the idea of being saved goes something like this. God created and loves humanity, but we have sinned. This sin separates us
from God and God's plan for our lives. God made provisions for our
sins by sending his son, Jesus, to die in vicarious punishment. By
accepting Jesus as Lord and savior of our lives, our relationships
with God can be restored, and we can be saved. That is, we can escape eternal punishment and go to heaven. Baptists expect every

adherent to make a public profession of accepting Jesus. This is done by walking down the church aisle at the end of a Sunday service during a period called the invitation. The choir sings music specifically meant to convince all in attendance of their sinfulness and need for Jesus's redemptive blood. This happens at the end of every service in the Baptist tradition, and it is usually a very emotional occasion. There are a lot of tears from the saved and his or her family. Once saved the expectation is that the Holy Spirit now lives in that person, and he or she will live a good Christian life. The person will behave, not ask too many questions, and spend the rest of his or her days trying to convince others their only way to heaven is to believe in God, sin, and God's plan of salvation.

I also have some less fond memories of those years as a Baptist. This was especially true near the end of those years before I finally decided I needed to move on. After twenty years of hearing the basic plan of salvation Sunday after Sunday after Sunday, I had gotten it. I began to wonder if there was anything else to learn there. Were there other things I could learn in this community about living an upright life and loving my neighbors? I started asking some pretty difficult questions. This was not a particularly welcome thing in a Baptist church. These were questions such as, "Why would a God who loves his children punish them for all eternity? Even lowly human beings are more loving to our children than that." Or, "Why does an all-powerful and all-loving God allow so much violence in the world?" However, it was probably this next question that was the most threatening. "If I am to love my neighbor as I love myself, wouldn't that love include a respect for my neighbor's religious traditions, values, and ideas?"

After a while the answers I received began to follow a pattern. A pattern that seemed to say, "We don't have an answer to that question. Therefore, we're not going to think about it or allow it to shape us in any way. We aren't going to accept any responsibility for the problems in the world." It is truly a nice, comfortable way to see life.

I moved on from this world view and this exclusive understanding of Christianity a long time ago, and I certainly feel it was a move in the right direction. Through all these years, I consciously moved on with my life and broadened my perspective to include other teachings from the Bible and insights from other faith traditions. I could not help but notice, though, how most of my friends and acquaintances from the Christian community, people who are basically of sound mind and good conscience, continued to be satisfied with that community and content within its narrow way of thinking. I'm continually intrigued about that. I'm also forever speculating about how I was so blessed to come into a more open, accepting way of seeing people from other faiths and cultures. Was it something about the composition of my soul that spurred me to seek and eventually find a much broader perspective, or was it something unique in my life's experience that led to my total dissatisfaction and disillusionment with the limited horizon of the Baptist church and its way of seeing the world?

It's not terribly difficult to understand why I felt a strong sense of community for many of my Baptist years given group dynamics. Groups where members understand and talk about things such as God and scripture using the same religious language and relying on the same traditional frames of reference have a high likelihood of fostering greater cohesiveness and camaraderie. In many senses of the word, the church of my formative years was very much a community. The sense of community it gives its members is self-reinforcing. Being a part of the community generates feelings of belonging, and those good feelings of connection make individual members reluctant to say or do anything outside the group's boundaries or commonly held beliefs. Members of such groups are deeply invested in their values and ways of seeing the world, and many are able to articulate and defend these values and beliefs in coherent, sophisticated ways. However, they are rarely capable of making the group itself and its way of understanding the world an object of reflection. That is, they are not capable of any objectivity when it comes to the very system of thought in which they are imbedded. Such systems are well circumscribed and few adventurous souls are capable of venturing outside the system and objectively critiquing it.

George Santayana said it well. "We cannot know who first discovered water. But we can be sure that it was not the fish." The fish are completely immersed and live their entire lives in a milieu totally unknown to them. Unable to jump out of the aquarium or ocean that contains them, they have no means of making the system they live in an object of scrutiny.

Santayana helped me gain some understanding and peace about my old friends in the Baptist church. He also helped me quit endlessly speculating about why so few ever dare venture out of the "blessed assurance, Jesus is mine" sort of mind-set. Just like a fish can't survive long outside its watery environs, so it is for the soul who dares leap beyond the confines of a community's tacit boundaries. Just like the fish that jumps outside the tank, that person who leaps gains a completely new and fascinating perspective on life in the community to which it belonged. But how disorienting and scary. It doesn't take the adventurous soul long to figure out that courageous leap has placed him or her in serious jeopardy. No longer totally immersed in the community's groupthink, he or she might soon (metaphorically) desiccate and die outside the group's supportive environment.

Santayana also helped me understand the dynamics of what happened to me when I flopped out of the aquarium, and I am deeply indebted to him for creating that very apt metaphor for this precipitous moment in my spiritual development. I flopped around for a long time trying to decide if I wanted to leap back into the fish tank of the Christian church community. In the end I decided it wasn't worth it. As much as I longed for acceptance and a restoration of solidarity and community, the cost was too high. It would have meant a sacrifice of integrity within my own soul. I stayed outside the community long enough to find some answers to my questions that were ultimately more rational, satisfying, and emotionally palatable. So I found my way into the fold of a more progressive faith tradition.

This might be a good place to stop. After all, if you're reading this book, then you're likely a progressive too, and haven't all of us religiously progressive types discovered water? We've made that gigantic leap out of the fishbowl of traditional religion and now see it for what it is. So why not just stop there and leave ourselves feeling smug and secure in our cosmopolitan perspectives?

I want to press Santayana's metaphor yet still further. There is a more serious message here for all of us if we stay with the metaphor and continue to use our imagination.

The fish out of water has a completely new perspective but few options to survive. It has to return to its world. If it gets back to water, it has three options. It can rejoin its community and pretend as if nothing happened. It can tell others about water and endure the snickers, taunts, and jeers that it will undoubtedly be subjected to, or it can go it alone. It can search for other fish that have had the outside experience and form a little community of those who have discovered this truth and survived.

There is a fourth option for that fish, though. Once the fish is back in the water, it can find its way back to those it swam with previously. It doesn't have to share its discovery with the other fish other than by conveying its newfound perspective through the way it lives its life. This is way of the mystic. Jesus told his followers to be in this world but not of this world because you are not of this world even as I am not of this world. The Buddhist idea of the bod-hisattva is one who has attained enlightenment but chooses to post-pone eternal bliss and return to the world to teach others. There is a similar idea in most faith traditions. It is an old, old story—the idea of possessing a special knowledge or insight but sharing it in understated ways the uninitiated can understand and follow.

I would suggest this is the challenge. Whatever faith tradition you come from, perhaps there are values, principles, and ideas there that you still need to be immersed in. Maybe there are people in your community you could benefit from if you continue or renew your connection. There might be benefits for them as well.

* * *

five

Lessons from a Toolshed

*"On the Tree of Life there are two birds, fast friends.
One bird eats the fruit of the tree; the other bird,
not eating, watches."*
—A short parable from the Rig Veda

I am standing in a dark toolshed. However, it is midday outside, and the sun is shining brightly. Through a crack in the roof comes a sunbeam. From where I stand, that beam of light is the most striking thing in the toolshed, and it traces a path like a laser to illuminate a precise area on the wall. I can see the sunbeam as a discrete object. I can see the particles of dust floating through it. The objects that fall in the field of light are clearly visible. Everything else in the toolshed is shrouded in dark and only faintly visible.

Suppose I move, step into the beam of light, and look upward. Once my eyes adjust, the objects in the toolshed are no longer visible to me. However, I behold something quite different—the green leaves on a tree just above the toolshed and the sun about ninety million miles away. Looking at the beam, looking along the beam to

33

see what it illuminates, and turning to see where the beam comes from are three entirely different experiences.

After you understand how to make the distinction between these three approaches to a subject, examples of it are everywhere. The sunbeam can serve to illustrate the different ways people approach almost any subject in life—love, beauty, religion, or more. Take religion - the sunbeam serves to illustrate three ways people approach the subject. Some people only look along the distinctive beam of their own particular religion to see life or the way their religion illuminates the elements of their particular corners of the world. Others step back from the sunbeams of their religious faiths and attempt to see the sunbeams objectively for what they are. They might become fascinated with sunbeams in general and compare them to other sunbeams. They might attempt to understand all their aspects using the various lenses of theology, psychology, or even political theory. The salient point is they stay outside the sunbeams and attempt to understand them. Still others will dare to step into the sunbeams, turn around, and look to see if they can determine anything about the sources of the beams. When this courageous approach is taken to the sunbeam of religion, it can lead to great depths of insight and commitment.

I am indebted to C. S. Lewis's essay "Meditation in a Toolshed" for the basic idea of this description.° Though, I have paraphrased and expanded upon his idea slightly.

Once the imagination is engaged and the basic differences in these three ways of experiencing the sunbeam has been grasped, a question arises. Which is the true or most accurate way of experiencing the sunbeam? The question has haunted and daunted humankind from the beginning, but never more than for the past one hundred years or so. This is because we live in a time and age when the answer has pretty much been taken for granted. In the modern way of thinking, stepping outside a subject is the only way to reliably know and understand it. Science has made tremendous strides in helping understand and manipulate the material world. Science is in large measure responsible for teaching people to always rely on objectivity first and foremost. When it comes to the material world, the scientific method and its reliance on empirical data gained through the five senses has taught people so much and offered the capacity and power to completely transform the world. Science is wonderful—as far as it goes. In the realm of physical objects, being objective and dealing only with empirical data are indeed taken for granted as the only reliable ways to study.

What about the rest of the world, though? Is there anyone who would disagree that the physical, material world comprises only a tiny fragment of a much larger universe? As far as significance to the experience of life, how much more important are things such as love, beauty, virtue, honor, and commitment? Can these things be known and understood by studying them in the same way one would dissect a frog or look at the images produced by an electron microscope? If people collect enough facts about the intangibles, can they claim mastery of the subjects?

Take love. Someone says he or she has studied all about love. The person knows the history of all the great love affairs from Antony and Cleopatra to Brad and Angelina. The person knows all the biology and physiology of the male and female organisms and the hormonal effects physical attraction induce. The person has read all Shakespeare's sonnets and Byron's poems. This person, however, has never been in love. Can this person claim to know what love is? Looking at the sunbeam of love from the outside is a completely inadequate way to know and understand the subject. Conversely take a young man or woman who is in love. That person can only look along the sunbeam at his or her beloved, and everything seems wonderful. There is magic everywhere for a person in love, and it transforms everything the lover sees and experiences about the object of his or her affection. Only after marriage or commitment might it begin to dawn on that person what the other is really like—manipulative, immature, or just plain selfish. Looking along the beam of love is also an inadequate way to know the subject. It is easy for things to deceive when seen only from the inside. However, who can claim to know anything about love who has not at least once been head over heels, totally immersed, and completely smitten with another?

I belabor this point for a reason. As it was pointed out to me recently, the assumptions and expectations of modern scientific and academic methods have deeply affected the study of religion.[P] It is assumed without discussion that a true account of religion must be obtained not from religious people but anthropologists, sociologists, or psychologists—those who look only at the sunbeam of religion. These people have stepped aside to a corner of the toolshed marked academia to offer external, objective analysis of the sunbeam. People are convinced an accurate picture is only possible from here. Never mind this perspective often refutes, debunks, or demythologizes what those inside the beam see. Objective, academic types tell us all those transcendent experiences that look so good and beautiful from inside are merely a conglomeration of biological instincts or the natural tendency of groups to stick together and tell each other the same myths to reinforce group identity.

Forget those of mystical mind-sets who claim to have actually turned and looked back as they attempt to glimpse and understand the sunbeam's source. Obviously they are even more deluded. Those external to the sunbeam insist the source is unknowable by any trustworthy capacity of human beings such as the five senses or any other verifiable method.

This assumption has infiltrated thinking and is so reinforced by academic institutions that it might be difficult to ever disengage from its limitations again. Consider this. In any reputable academic institution, scholars who can discuss religion from a historical, cultural, behavioral, psychological, or sociological view naturally dominate the religious studies program. The subject is studied almost exclusively from the perspective of people who are very good at looking at the sunbeam but not necessarily from the perspective of those who are good at looking along it. In the formal academic study of religion in most colleges and universities, there is a huge assumption that modern science has a lock on knowledge.

I say this in full awareness of why religion is so often kept at arm's length. Look no further than the rabid religious cults of Jonestown or Heaven's Gate to see how easily and deeply people can be deceived when they see things only as insiders and in the narrow light of such a perspective. Does it necessarily have to be so, though?

My generation and the one or two preceding it have lived with and become completely accustomed to the split between religion and science. Those generations have labored under the assumption that the modern methods of thought are the only reliable ways to understand something. Unfortunately in practice this often means the serious student of a subject such as religion limits himself or herself to the verifiable. Intangibles such as moral values or aesthetic judgments are completely off the radar screen. Ask yourself if someone can study the beauty of a symphony or painting. Can one document the love of a mother for her child? Of course not. These things are beyond the limits of empirical knowledge. Therefore, it becomes accepted practice to simply ignore them in any serious study.

If the questions religion tackles (questions of meaning and right and wrong) were simply matters of belief or faith, then it would be OK to ignore them. Human beings, however, can come to know the difference between right and wrong in a given society at a given time, and many virtues transcend societies and time periods. All major religions teach these perennially true values. Therefore, even though moral values are intangible, there are ways of coming to know them.

To come to know what religious faith is all about and to come to some realization of its true meaning and significance, one must enter fully into it. One must dare to move beyond looking at the sunbeam and look along it. One must step into the community as part of it and do more than just imagine what it would be like to emulate the members. To do so generates an *entirely* different perspective.

Whether dealing with a civic club, a sports team, or a political organization, one can't come to any true realization about the members or what they are all about until one participates. There are many levels of participation. One could go one or twice a month, go all the time, or even go so far as to become an officer or board member.

When it comes to a religious community, I would define participation a bit differently. I mentioned earlier that if religion was merely a matter of belief or faith, then it would be okay to ignore any other way of knowing it than dispassionately studying it from a safe corner of the toolshed. However, religion is more than a matter of faith or belief. It is about actually having an experience of the religion and its community. It is about experience and even transformation.

* * *

six

The Holy Grail of Religious Authority

The legend of the Holy Grail is one of the most beloved, enduring stories in Western literature. According to the classic story, the Holy Grail was the cup Jesus used at the Last Supper. Soon after the Passion, Jesus's great-uncle, Joseph of Arimathea, received the cup to collect Jesus's blood while he tended to Jesus during and after the crucifixion. After Jesus's death Joseph was imprisoned in a rock tomb. Joseph was left there to starve, but the magical power of the Grail provided him with fresh food and drink every day and sustained him for several years. When released Joseph traveled to Britain, and the Grail was taken to Corbenic where it was housed in a spectacular castle. As the years and generations passed, the Grail Kings (descendants of Joseph) guarded the cup.

Eventually all forgot the location of this great castle. However, centuries later the Grail came into prominence again. During the time of King Arthur, the Knights of the Round Table were all famished and waiting for a great banquet, but Arthur declared the meal couldn't be served until an adventure occurred. The Knights were then given this grand vision of angels descending from heaven and carrying the Grail. They were not allowed to actually see the Grail, however, as a cloth covered it. Everyone was in rapture at this magnificent spectacle, but suddenly it vanished. Sir Gawain proposed that all knights present take a vow that they will go in pursuit of the Grail to behold it unveiled. Further, it was prophesied that the best and noblest knight in the land would find the Grail in a wild and desolate part of Britain. Whenever this knight fulfilled the great quest and found the Grail, the Grail King would be healed, and the desolate land would be restored to life. The Grail quest became the highest and noblest goal of the Knights of the Round Table.

They roamed the country looking for it and had many adventures along the way. Parzival found the castle and the Grail King but failed to ask for the Grail. Next Lancelot came close to fulfilling the quest. However, because of his love for and adultery with Guinevere, King Arthur's queen, he was deemed not noble enough and ultimately denied access to the Grail. Finally Galahad, Lancelot's son, arrived and was sufficiently noble and pure of heart to gain the Grail. The Grail King was healed, life was restored to the kingdom, and Galahad was lifted up to heaven.

At its heart the quest for the Holy Grail is about authority. The story grew out of the situation in medieval England where people were required to hold religious beliefs imposed on them by an outside authority—the church. This made the entire culture a wasteland. According to mythologist Joseph Campbell, everyone was leading "inauthentic lives." They held positions they inherited and did not earn, professed love to arranged spouses, and claimed belief in a religion from another part of the world (the Middle East) that the far-off Roman church imposed on them. This made it a land where people lived inauthentic lives, accepted outside authority, and did as they were told. No one had any courage to go and search for themselves.[9]

Coming to terms with authority presents a challenge at every developmental stage of human beings. Children are under the authority of their parents. At some point, though, everyone must separate from parents and their rules, demands, and expectations to become a fully autonomous adult. However, in making a way into the world, one must train for a vocation and place oneself under the authority of teachers and educational institutions. After entering the workplace, there are even more authority figures in the forms of bosses and supervisors. In civil society there are local, state, and national government authorities. Bending to the dictates of authority is an inherent part of the human experience, and humans have always had an uneasy relationship with it. Humans want, need, and even demand authority from leadership. Complex systems seem to function best when clear lines of authority and a chain of command exist. Humans can't seem to live without authority but are seldom happy with it. Authority is often abused, and experience teaches people to be suspicious of it.

Another authority that holds sway over people's lives is religious authority. Religious authority is said to come from four sources—tradition, scripture, reason, and experience. (These four sources are commonly known as the Wesleyan Quadrilateral, named for John Wesley, the founder of the Methodist Church and the first person to distinctly enumerate them.) For the first fifteen hundred years of the church's history, tradition was the primary source of religious authority. Authority came from the hierarchy headed by the pope. This structure was said to originate with Peter and be passed down to succeeding popes in apostolic succession. With the Protestant Reformation in the sixteenth century, the Western world moved toward scripture as the primary source of authority. Martin Luther summarized this position, which later became known as *sola scriptura*, when he uttered this pithy remark. "The simplest layman armed with scripture is greater than the mightiest pope without it."

Then came the Enlightenment in the eighteenth century, and reason increasingly became a reliable foundation for religious authority. The rise of humanism and the humanistic tendencies in many existing religious traditions speak to this. The nineteenth century witnessed experience becoming a wellspring for religious authority. Pentecostalism, with its emphasis on the direct experience of God, became a specific religious movement along with the traditions of Unitarianism and Universalism. Ralph Waldo Emerson, a former Unitarian minister, began his essay "Nature" with, "The foregoing generations beheld God and nature face to face; we, through their eyes. Why should not we also enjoy an original relation to the universe?" This was his declaration of independence from the authority of anything other than his experience and intuition. As Emerson's biographer, Robert Richardson, declared, "The book 'Nature' is not designed as an appeal to earlier or other authority but as a self-evident, self-validating account."[R] With the publication of "Nature," Emerson was on his own quest to behold the holy grail of primal truth about himself and his relationship to the universe. The grail he uncovered and shared with the world through his seminal thoughts and writings made a substantial contribution to transcendentalism. This became the intellectual and spiritual foundation for modern Unitarianism.

The imaginative stories of the Grail quest arose out of twelfth-century Britain's need to find its own story in Jesus's Passion drama. Grail legends have many close parallels in Celtic myths. These tell tales of magic vessels that provided for the needs of all who drank and ate from them. Though Christianity was foreign to the indigenous culture, it somehow became a part of a new mythology through the creation of the Arthurian romance tales. The biblical story of the passion and Celtic folklore were woven together into a unique epic that represented an entire nation's spiritual yearnings. The storytellers and mythmakers of medieval Britain composed the multifaceted Grail lore that simultaneously appropriated and rebelled against Christianity. (Rebellion in the sense of resistance to the institutional authority of the Church in Rome.) Ultimately the Grail story is about the courageous individual searching for spiritual meaning in a barren religious landscape. The religious institution makes it barren by controlling and subduing the human desire for fulfillment only available through a personalized belief system.

Consider these lines in *Parzival*—one of the most popular versions of the Grail quest. "They thought it would be a disgrace to go forth as a group. Each entered the forest at a point that he himself had chosen where it was darkest and there was no path."⁵ Reaching spiritual maturity requires us to make our own paths. If you are on an established path, it is already someone else's, and you are not trusting your own authority.

In one of the many versions of the Grail quest, Parzival finally finds the castle at the end of an arduous journey, and he encounters the Grail King. The king is wounded and brought in on a litter. Parzival's compassion moves him to want to ask questions and find out what happened to the wounded king. However, Parzival has been brought up and trained in the ways of a proper knight, and a good knight does not ask questions. So he represses his inner questing spirit, and the adventure fails. Years later, after many more trials and learning experiences sufficiently teach him to trust himself and his own authority, Parzival can finally return to the castle of the wounded Grail King and heal him.

In medieval times the Grail story developed to breathe new life into the traditional church's tired story of the crucifixion's aftermath. Today the Grail quest has been endlessly appropriated to give credence to all sorts of new age ideas and mystical movements. This includes everything from Dan Brown's theories of Mary Magdalene as the mother of Jesus's child to the feminine spirituality of *The Mists of Avalon* to the raucous antics of *Monty Python and the Holy Grail*.

Perhaps you can also find yourself in the story. The world today is not so different than the one that prompted the bards of medieval England to compose these stories. Today's religious landscape is just as barren. It is still populated by people who rely almost exclusively on tradition and literal scriptural interpretation to provide the authoritative source of meaning and purpose for their lives. This can be quite seductive for those who long for security and clear-cut answers to life's ups and downs. Many take comfort and shelter in the pat answers and dogma that constitute institutional Christian faith. To have "the Bible says" at the ready whenever life's injustices and uncertainties threaten to overwhelm certainly has its appeal. The day eventually comes, however, when the neatness of this approach no longer works. The whole system built on an unquestioned external authority comes crashing down. Eventually experience does not mesh with the interpretations offered through religious institutions, and disillusion is the inevitable result.

Contrast this with the examples of the courageous, noble souls of the Knights of the Round Table who quested alone and found meaning in the search itself. Their stories reveal the maturing of spirit that occurred as they quested after the elusive grail. The knights acted out of their own courage and their own authority, much like today's progressive religious seekers who rely on the authority of reason and personal experience.

Ever since I first read about King Arthur and the Knights of the Round Table as a young boy, the mystery of the Holy Grail has fascinated me. What was it? Where could it possibly be hidden? Why was the Grail believed to hold these mystical, magical powers? The element of mystery that surrounded the whole idea was part of my fascination. The mystery made the stories compelling and induced me to aspire to the virtues of the knights—loyalty, honor, bravery, and concern for the weak and less fortunate. The way the stories capture the imagination and invite readers to contemplate the

Grail's mysterious aspects seem to account for a great deal of the story's enduring appeal.

Scott Peck suggests, "There are some who are attracted to religion in order to approach mystery, while there are others who are attracted to religion in order to escape from mystery."[T] Religious mysteries are not like scientific mysteries or murder mysteries—things that can be solved with enough facts and examination. The mysteries of religious faith (the nature of God, truth, love, the self, and the universe) are not solvable in the traditional sense. The mystery only deepens with contemplation. This does not mean people should not reflect upon these things just because they are unfathomable. It means people need to bring more than the powers of reason and logical analysis to bear upon them. People gain understanding through living these mysteries. People come to know themselves more fully as they live and experience themselves in different situations. The stories generated as humans explore that mystery are part of the wisdom gained. That is how the mystery of the Grail functions in the stories it generated and continues to generate from the human imagination.

The quest for the Holy Grail is ultimately a story about the noble individual acting on personal authority beyond the institutional church and its priests. The sincere religious seeker returns to this issue continually. He or she weighs the answers provided by tradition and scripture against the authority gained by learning to trust his or her heart and reflecting on personal experience. Perhaps as one who senses the restorative power contained in the faculties of heart and mind, you too can bring life back to a barren world. If so, you might also find solace from these colorful, quixotic stories of knights in search of the Holy Grail.

* * *

Part II

—

Faith

seven

Questioning Faith

"The supreme function of reason is to show man that some things are beyond reason."
—Blaise Pascal

Mark Twain once quipped, "Faith is believing something that you know ain't true." There is a certain humor in that remark because it brings to mind some of the preposterous things people accept in the name of religion. A bit of skepticism is often justified when it comes to what passes as religious "faith." However, there's a double entendre in this chapter's title. Doubt, questioning, and skepticism aren't necessarily the opposite of faith but can actually be elements of a mature faith. Here is a story that helps illuminate what faith is and isn't.

Tightrope walking was highly celebrated in the nineteenth century. Tightrope walkers were the daredevils of that era. Those who had the nerve to attempt walks over vast expanses or great heights and had a flair for adding a few theatrics to their stunts could attract Super Bowl–type crowds. Probably the most famous tightrope walker of all time is Charles Blondin. He owed most of his celebrity and fortune to walking across a tightrope stretched over the span of Niagara Falls. He first accomplished this feat on June 30, 1859.

He went on to perform this feat many times, and he added another daring element each time to attract new crowds. He crossed one time on stilts, once on a bicycle, once in the dark, and once pushing a wheelbarrow full of rocks. Once he even stopped in the middle and cooked an omelet on a portable stove. The most interesting dramatic flair he added to his stunt, however, was after he walked across the falls once and reached the other side. He whipped the crowd into an enthusiastic frenzy by asking them repeatedly if they believed he could do it again. Their shouts of "yes" got louder and louder. Then he asked them if they believed he could carry a person across the falls on his back. Again they chanted "yes." After a slight pause, he then asked the crowd who among them wanted to go first. The great multitude fell silent.

Ministers in evangelical churches have recounted this story thousands of times to illustrate the difference between belief and faith. The crowd believed in Blondin. They believed he could accomplish the feat he proposed because they had seen him do equally difficult things with their own eyes. However, none had the faith to hop on his back and make the trip across the falls. The analogy between belief in Blondin and his achievement and belief in Jesus and his great accomplishments is a clever one. By drawing such a sharp distinction between belief and faith, the preacher's strategy is to beckon the congregation toward a deeper commitment to Jesus. The church members might step out in faith, put their trust in him, and be more devoted to the church.

The analogy is effective, but the story also shrewdly points out a vital difference between the two concepts of belief and faith. It's one thing to believe something—to affirm a reasoned opinion about the merit of an idea or about the ability or trustworthiness of a person. It's another thing entirely to have faith—to fully commit and courageously step out wherever ideals or courageous leaders might compel. The story makes a vivid distinction between enthusiastic intellectual agreement with a thought or idea and being willing to put oneself metaphorically out there on the tightrope or, by analogy, "out there" in the really difficult work that following Jesus or some other great moral teacher would demand.

This distinction is certainly a worthwhile one and can lead to serious reflection on what real trust and commitment involve. The message here resonates because the world is overflowing with religious ideologies. We weary of them because we see little evidence they lead to changed lives. Cynicism grows because we observe that members of these groups don't seem to lead their lives according to the ideals they espouse. Most importantly, though, the story invites us to revisit the values we acknowledge and give voice to. It might even challenge us to do some inventory of our own convictions and to question whether we could marshal the courage to step out during a serious challenge and act upon the ideals and values we claim. In one sense of religious faith and what it encompasses, this story is quite illuminating. It defines the particular meaning of faith as trust—putting one's life in the hands of a person, idea, or institution.

However, for some the word "faith" is an anathema. For some faith means accepting some proposition based solely on the word of an authoritative scripture, institution, or person. It means refusing to engage powers of reason or the faculty for doubt and skepticism. When those people hear a story such as the one about Blondin used as an illustration of faith, it is completely off-putting. It's as if faith means giving credence to some kind of derring-do or parlor trick such as what Blondin pulled off or some other sleight of hand, and it seems totally inconsistent with being a rational, enlightened individual in twenty-first-century America.

What preachers attempt to do when they use stories such as this is to elevate the concept of faith above the concept of belief. However, what they usually end up doing is cheapening the idea of faith. They make faith into an act of surrender or bravado based on a childlike credulity in a person who appears to have formidable powers or in an idea that seems to defy reason. It's much like the idea of having faith in Jesus simply because he allegedly performed miracles. Unitarian minister George Ripley was attempting to elevate faith beyond simple credulity in the face of awe when he said that faith does not depend on a belief in miracles but rather belief in miracles depends on faith. There was nothing miraculous about what Blondin did, but the idea is the same. Faith is more than trusting someone simply because one believes he or she has some formidable power.

Religious faith is always concerned with what really matters in life. As the theologian Paul Tillich described it, our faith is what is of ultimate concern for us. No illustration or example of faith will work unless it concerns the ultimate value and meaning to a human life. Let's look again at this story of Blondin. Say there was some adventurous soul in the crowd who stepped forward and accepted Blondin's challenge to be transported back across the gorge. He or she would have demonstrated "faith" in Blondin in the sense that he or she believed he could do it, and that person was willing to demonstrate that conviction through actions. Crossing the gorge, however, is by no means a matter of ultimate concern for this person. He or she is just someone willing to take a dare. The action is not likely to lead to a changed life (unless Blondin stumbles and they both fall to their deaths). Stepping out and trusting Blondin to carry him or her across the gorge will no more bring meaning to that person's life than simply trusting Jesus. Belief and trust in Jesus changes nothing unless the person is willing to follow his teachings and make faith an action by living life in accordance to those teachings. Therefore, "faith" (in a religious context) can be used in two completely different, almost contradictory ways. This leads to all manner of confusion.

Why does this confusion exist? Part of the reason is laziness in the use of the words "faith" and "belief." Most use the words interchangeably. For instance, the statement, "His belief is that God exists" doesn't change materially if phrased, "His faith is that God exists."

The words don't mean the same thing, though. A belief is an opinion. One might believe something rather casually. "I believe it's going to rain today." Also one might have a deep emotional investment in a belief. "I believe a good, loving God couldn't possibly have had anything to do with the death of your baby." Regardless of the depth of emotion, beliefs are still a construction of the mind. Belief is an intellectual enterprise. The mind might go to great lengths or possibly even construct illogical beliefs in an attempt to give some sense of integrity and coherence to the inner life.

When people find out I'm a Universalist minister, I get asked all sorts of interesting questions. The way they frame their questions is a source of fascination for me. They don't start by asking how I understand life, what my ritual life is like, or what my values are. What they usually turn to is belief. What do I believe? At a party the host once asked me pointedly if I believed in God. I usually try to put a humorous spin on my answer to such a question in an attempt to bring some levity to what could become a rather tense conversation when I am questioned in such a way. However, in this case I could tell this person wasn't going to allow me to change the tone of our interaction. Therefore, I responded, "The problem I have goes much deeper than that. It's not a question of whether or not I believe in God. The problem I have is that I don't believe in belief." Well, that put an end to our conversation. I doubt if he will invite me to any more parties.

Belief is one thing. Faith, on the other hand, is something much deeper and more elemental to who we are. Faith is our orientation to life and our way of engaging in the world. It encompasses hopes, and it manifests ultimate concerns. Under this understanding, faith is universal to the human experience. It doesn't have to be overtly religious. Every person has faith—a way he or she orients to the reality of existence and a way to construct meaning. Everyone has an ultimate concern whether or not that ultimate concern ever finds expression in a religious community or institution.

Why is it important to recognize belief and faith as separate? I'll give you three reasons. First, it helps people make some sense of the incongruities in others when the faith they express through actions doesn't line up with the beliefs they claim to hold. Everyone has encountered examples of this. When people don't live up to the beliefs they claim to have, there's a word for it—hypocrisy. A boss claims he operates his business ethically, but he cheats his customers when he gets a chance. A friend is frequently hurt by his partner's sexual affairs and flirtatious behavior, but she always declares her husband to be the only one for her. The list goes on and on. The walk just doesn't jive with the talk. People's faith, as demonstrated by their actions, is not consistent with their professed beliefs.

Second, it serves people well in coming to know and understand themselves better and to grow spiritually. Having a strong faith is so often equated with certainty. However, having complete certainty about the things one hopes for and the desires of the heart is not faith. That is denial sometimes bordering on delusion or, in many respects, some kind of self-hypnosis. Faith is not the absence of doubt. Faith is having enough confidence in the guidance of the heart that one can honor doubts and be open to new beliefs and possibilities. People who live behind the pretense that they don't have any doubts appear completely hypocritical to those humble and honest enough to admit that life is uncertain. At best people have only incomplete answers. Worse yet, people who construct these facades of complete certainty end up being hypocrites to themselves because inwardly they know they are living a lie. When people are certain about something, they stop taking in new information. This can only lead to stagnation. It's better for spiritual growth and development when faith is open ended and allows further questions and people don't have to stick to the stale, worn-out ideas of a church or religious tradition that may no longer work.

Third, clarifying and elevating the idea of faith while diminishing the importance of belief makes for so many more possibilities in interfaith dialogue and cooperation. People from different denominations and religions often have widely different beliefs. As diverse as their beliefs might be, though, many times those of goodwill from different religions have remarkably similar faith. Joseph Campbell loved to tell stories of encounters between Buddhist monks and Catholic monks who found much in common around faith because of their common participation in the contemplative life. How these monks could get along so well was a mystery to both the Catholic and Buddhist laities, many of whom saw differing beliefs as an obstacle to meaningful conversation.

I experienced something similar to those monks in the course of my church's work with Habitat for Humanity. We came together with people from other churches in the area, and I doubt if we could have found enough common ground among our beliefs to even begin a civil conversation about religion or theology. However, we had a similar faith. We all knew that a concern for those who didn't have decent roofs over their heads went to the heart of what our religious communities could and should be about. Doesn't this better reflect the values and what is of ultimate concern to religious communities than any set of professed beliefs ever could?

For those of a religiously progressive mind-set who live more by faith than the words of some creed, it's very frustrating to be asked about specific beliefs. That frustration encapsulates the difference between belief and faith. When asked this question, there's so much I desire to express about our church community, and it simply can't be expressed as a list of ideas or propositions we've adopted or hold in common. Faith is the ongoing, creative process by which people confront and deal with the ambiguities of life and attempt to meet its challenges. Faith is about a way of experiencing life and investing it with meaning despite its difficulties, tragedies, and pain. There's simply no way to express anything close to that by giving a list of opinions about the existence of a supreme being or about the authority of some person, book, or set of writings. If only people would ask me about what I love, what the experience of my church community is like, or where we invest our time and energy. I would be much better able to express myself and do justice to what we are about. Those ways of framing conversations are so much more engaging and energizing, and they get so much closer to the essence of what I mean when I use the word "faith."

Faith (or really any other word) fails to describe this confusing, confounding, exciting, mysterious journey we are on together. Perhaps the best we can do is live our faith in such a way that others will become curious about us and maybe even be enticed by the way we give meaning to this crazy gift of life we have been given.

* * *

eight

Transforming Faith

Many people equate the words "belief" and "faith," and this causes no end of problems for non-creedal faith traditions, i.e., traditions that don't unite people around certain beliefs or creeds. Faith and belief aren't the same thing. Faith has much deeper, richer connotations—something that's been referred to as "faith beyond belief." Belief is an intellectual enterprise; faith is something more primal to who we are as human beings. Faith is concerned with the ways we endow our lives with meaning. It's a creative process and can't always be named. Faith originates more from the heart than the head and is an expression of values, transcendent hopes, and desires. The radical difference between faith and belief is dramatized in the literary work *Saint Manuel the Good, Martyr*.

Manuel is the priest in a small Spanish village in the nineteenth century. The townspeople adore him because of his gentleness and the great good he does. Often he serves the people in unassuming ways. Instead of refusing a holy burial to someone who committed suicide as the institutional Catholic church insists, Manuel conducts the rite and explains that he knows the person would have repented in those last moments. When a woman returns to the village bearing an illegitimate child, he quietly convinces her old boyfriend to marry her so she can live without shame and the child will have a father.

One day a young man named Lazarus returns home from the New World to his native Spanish village after a long absence because he finds out his mother is dying. He is at her bedside with Manuel, and his mother grabs Lazarus's hand and asks him to pray for her. Lazarus does not answer his mother, but as they leave the room, he tells Manuel he wants to pray for his mother but cannot because he doesn't believe in God. "That's nonsense," Manuel replies. "You don't have to believe in God to pray."[U] So Lazarus promises his mother he will pray for her. He does, and this allows her to die in peace. After this Lazarus continues to pray. He begins to participate in the religious life of the village, and he even takes communion. Lazarus's act so touches Manuel that the priest begins to spend time with Lazarus. They take walks by the lake as they converse over the nature of religion and the meaning of faith. Manuel becomes a mentor to Lazarus, and Manuel eventually confesses that he doesn't believe in many Christian tenets either such as the afterlife. He confides in Lazarus that he's not even sure he believes in God. Lazarus asks the priest how he can continue to fulfill his duties if he doesn't believe. The priest tells Lazarus that the church's teachings might or might not be true. Regardless of what he personally believes, though, those tenets give the people comfort and happiness. They are, therefore, good things, so he has and will continue to fulfill his priestly office. Manuel eventually dies, and Lazarus takes Manuel's place in serving the people of the village until his own death.[V]

The priest in this story clarifies the difference between belief and faith rather distinctly. He takes belief out of the religious equation entirely. The story's author was a Spaniard named Miguel de Unamuno. He used the priest in this story to depict a life lived for the sake of faith itself and unhampered by the mental baggage of belief. Even though Unamuno wrote the story in 1930, its message resonates even more powerfully today.

Our world is more polarized than ever. Every institution and system draws lines between believers and unbelievers. Religious leaders consolidate power by highlighting the differences in people's beliefs. In virtually every town across America, dozens of churches promote the idea that their particular way of believing in God is the correct one. Meanwhile the new atheist authors—Sam Harris, Richard Dawkins, and Christopher Hitchens—are writing some of the best-selling contemporary books. These authors insist that belief in God is responsible for virtually all the modern world's ills.

The priest in Unamuno's story transcends the beliefs of traditional religiosity. As with any priest, people would certainly hope he's further along in his spiritual development than his parishioners. Manuel demonstrates this quite effectively as he ministers to his flock in profound ways. However, what really captivated me about this story is the way the priest also demonstrates that his spiritual development goes beyond the whole religious system. Rather than get hung up on his disagreements with Catholicism and its doctrines prohibiting funeral rites and burial for suicide victims or its treatment of a child born out of wedlock, he operates a ministry of love, compassion, worth, and dignity while conducting his priestly functions within the system and rules of the institutional church. Unamuno's priest circumvents church doctrine regarding suicide and illegitimacy. Manuel pays no attention to the complex belief system these harsh teachings create. The faith by which the priest lives and acts eclipses his personal doubts, and it also finds a way to love when there is nothing to point the way. Neither the principles fostered by church teaching nor the prevailing beliefs of his community are of any use to him in discerning the loving thing to do. Despite all this he yet finds a way.

So often in the process of growing up spiritually, the tendency is to get hung up on skepticism and doubt. All religious institutions present a bewildering array of doctrines, teachings, and beliefs. At some point in our lives and development, if we are fully functional adults capable of independent thought, it's quite natural to begin reflecting on these doctrines and beliefs and to examine them in the light of growing wisdom. In this process we might ask a series of questions about them. Are they consistent with our life experiences? Are they affirming of who I am as a person of worth and dignity? Do they bring meaning and integrity to relationships and allow us to love our neighbors? While questions often threaten institutions and the less reflective people who inhabit them, it's a good and necessary thing to have some capacity to hold these doctrines and beliefs at arm's length. This helps us grow and develop as spiritual beings. As the theologian Paul Tillich put it, doubt is not the opposite of faith. It is an element of faith.[w]

Having a skeptical and questioning posture about prevailing beliefs is a necessary step on the way to greater spiritual maturity. According to Scott Peck, James Fowler, and others, the need to be skeptical and assert individuality is necessary for spiritual growth. However, as I've thought more and more about this, I've come to see some weaknesses in their stage theories of spiritual growth. Peck's theory describes four stages of spiritual growth: Stage I being chaotic, antisocial, stage II is formal, institutional, stage III is skeptic, individual, and stage IV is mystic, communal. According to Peck growth from stage II to stage III is a conversion and "we neither can nor should skip over questioning in our development."[x] Fowler's theory describes six stages of faith; his Stage 4 being the salient one to skepticism and questioning. Fowler, like Peck, insists that a person has to become a Stage 4 reflective on their way to fuller faith develoment. "For a genuine move to Stage 4 to occur there must be an interruption of reliance on external sources of authority.":"Y

It is necessary that at some point people individuate from many of the rigidities of traditional religiosity. It's often refreshing and freeing to discover fallacies in some things parents and traditions have asserted. However, because it affirms skepticism when people awaken to these fallacies, it's easy to get stuck there. When people find reason to fault some of the beliefs of an institution such as the church, it's all too easy to throw everything out. People become a little too comfortable assuming skeptical postures. People can become a little too smug or even a little too cynical. Perhaps making skepticism into a discrete stage of spiritual growth isn't the most constructive label for what happens when people reflect and question. (In subsequent chapters I will draw upon the wisdom of Peck and Fowler's stages and I am indebted to their work. My contribution to this subject takes two tracts – first, more of a focus on the emotional process involved in faith development by sharing examples and reflections from my own journey, and second, illustrating the types of great leaders that all the stages can produce.)

The story of St. Manuel is instructive here as well. Manuel's protégé, Lazarus, is representative of skepticism. He's been off to the New World. He's experienced other lands. He's more cosmopolitan. He's experienced other cultures and ways of thinking. He finds the religious views in his old hometown quaint and provincial; they no longer work for him. He says he can't pray for his mother because he no longer believes in the way the townspeople believe.

Manuel's response is quick and to the point. Belief in God is not necessary for Lazarus to pray for his mother. Manuel has doubts about the existence of God, and yet this doesn't deter him from encouraging Lazarus to pray. On the contrary, the fact he's been where Lazarus is in his own faith journey gives him the authority to speak forcefully to Lazarus. He can unflinchingly advocate prayer as a way for Lazarus to affirm his love for his mother.

There was a time in my life when I found comfort and even affirmation in the idea that agnosticism and doubt were necessary for me to grow spiritually. Given the increasing importance placed on belief in Western religious culture and the dysfunctions that creates, perhaps it is necessary to go through a distinct period of holding those beliefs at arm's length. However, I've known many people who have more open-minded, enlightened views of our diverse world. These people can accept others from different religions and feel no compulsion to fix or convert them, and these individuals never left the church or went through rejections of it to come around to these more progressive views. One can get perspective on the real heart of Christianity or any other religion without having to go into full rebellion. There are, therefore, many paths to a mature faith.

It's not necessary to turn to fiction to find an example of someone who lived a life of faith and took belief out of the religious equation. There is the real-life example of Mother Teresa and what came to light about her inner life soon after her death. During her long life, Mother Teresa wrote many letters to her superiors and to those to whom she confessed. Not long after she died in 1997, a collection of these letters was published. Many contained confessions that for much of her life, including most of the time she worked with the poor in Calcutta, she harbored doubts about the existence of God. Her posthumous confession led to an interesting public debate about whether she should be considered a hypocrite. It's ironic that someone who lived a saintly life of faith but secretly had doubts would have the word "hypocrite" attached to him or her.[2] This just goes to show how far off base society has gone in regard to defining people by their beliefs.

All definitions of faith seem to come up short. However, there is one that gets very close to the meaning I'm trying to get at. The best definition of faith I know is *that which makes us whole*. It is that which gives meaning and integrity to our lives. In the New Testament "wholeness" means very much the same thing as "holiness." Wholeness is also equated with healing. The Greek words for "healing," "wholeness," and "holiness" all derive from the same root word. Jesus understood faith as that which makes us whole. When it was reported he had healed someone, Jesus would say to that person, "Your faith has made you whole."[6] As Jesus understood it, faith was about a way of seeing life that gave wholeness, meaning, and purpose to existence. Following Jesus's usage, faith is better understood as a process than as something humans possess. It's something people do rather than have. In the sense Jesus used it, faith is a verb rather than a noun.

I've experienced the difference between belief and faith rather poignantly in my marriage. Kathy and I have very different beliefs about God, about the spiritual significance of the Christhood associated with the historical person of Jesus, and about an afterlife and the possibilities of what that might be like. However, we have very similar faiths. Using faith as a verb, we faith life quite similarly. We agree that life is always worth living despite pain, and every moment is to be savored. We put much importance on being grateful for what we've been privileged to have together and the experiences we've shared. We don't look for reasons to be sad or bitter. These things are the very heart and substance of faith. With these things in common, what does it matter our beliefs are different?

The Hindus have a word for faith that also gets to its essence. That word is "sraddha." It translates to "to set one's heart on." What a beautiful phrase. It suggests that faith is an initiative that comes

6 Mark 5:34.

from the heart—the very center of existence. It also hints at challenge. It suggests that faith involves change or movement. Having faith means being set on becoming, growing into, or achieving something. It has nothing to do with the right thoughts or opinions. It's an alignment of one's heart with the heart of life and the heart of the universe.

* * *

nine

Stages of Faith Development

My years in college were eye-opening. I learned the value of questioning. In my biology and chemistry classes, I was introduced to the scientific method. This is basically learning how to learn. To learn something in science, one asks a question. Then one tries to come up with answers to that question. To confirm the answer is correct, one runs tests. Asking questions is how people learn.

As I look back on those formative years, though, the questions I asked in biology class did not open my eyes so much as the ones I began to ask about life, meaning, and purpose. I was curious about a lot more than viruses, bacteria, quasars, and lasers. I wanted to know more about religion and values. This was especially true since my college experience was exposing me to a much more diverse humanity than I had ever experienced. Some of the cast of characters around me held very different beliefs than mine, and some of those beliefs made more sense than those I had acquired during my relatively conservative religious training. The question that especially stuck in my gut was the one about other religions. Traditional Christianity teaches that salvation is only available through believing certain things about the person of Jesus who is unique in being the Christ. The conclusion that people of other faiths who do not have such a belief are condemned to hell inevitably results from this teaching.

Two things convinced me this simply could not be the way of things. First, a loving God would not condemn people simply because they had been born in other parts of the world and raised to believe something different than I had. That violated my sense of love and fairness. Second, the morals and behavior of many around me who observed these other religions were often superior to the morals and behavior of many of my Christian friends. This violated my sense of logic. All this simply did not compute. So I began to ask a lot of questions. I hypothesized that the correct answer might be that everything I had been taught might not be correct. In matters of God and religion, though, there is no way to test a hypothesis. However, there are reason and common sense, and it was these faculties of the human mind that told me this exclusive brand of Christian thought was simply not true.

I journeyed in traditional Christian circles many years during and after college, and I occasionally got the opportunity to explain why I did not buy into traditional ideas about salvation. When I did so, I got two distinct kinds of responses. Most people would immediately get defensive and start quoting scripture to me. This was the typical response. However, occasionally someone would acknowledge that he or she did not have all the answers either. After I collected enough of these experiences over the years, I realized there was a distinct barrier separating these two kinds of people—those with rigid, fixed perceptions about God and faith who could not step beyond that invisible wall and those who were not bound into this relatively narrow spiritual space and were not afraid to question and use their faculty of reason and emotional sense of fairness in reflecting on God. It's as if some people are secure enough in their faith and who they are to cross over a certain threshold, and some aren't.

One day I was having one of these conversations in a Sunday school class, and a man took it upon himself to straighten me out. A woman in the group named Marla chimed in and immediately silenced this man. Marla said, "It's OK to have doubts. God's a big boy. He doesn't need defending. He can look out for himself." She might or might not have gotten it right in her use of the male pronoun for God, but consider the power and intention of her words. When I heard them, I could immediately let go of my defensiveness. It became abundantly clear how this man and everyone else who felt the need for a strict understanding of God were actually boxed in to a limited world view. They were simply incapable of stepping over this threshold into a place of healthy skepticism.

In later conversations with Marla, I voiced my appreciation for the way she had corroborated and validated me and my doubts concerning the nature of God. On another occasion she made another pithy statement that has stayed with me throughout my life. She said, "Yes. It's OK to have doubts. Otherwise you are subject to people's unhealthy notions of God. But one day you will also discover there's power in learning to doubt your doubts. Only when you are capable of doubting your doubts will you find true freedom and take the next step on your spiritual journey."

I took serious note of what Marla said, but I simply was not ready to move beyond my doubts at that point. My doubts had rescued me from a stultifying, black-and-white religion, and I clung to my skepticism for many years. However, in 1988 I had an experience that was and is difficult to describe or label. Some effort must be made, though, so I am going to call it "community." It was really an experience of grasping a great mystery, and the intensity of it only lasted a few days, but it left a mark on my life that has persisted until this day.

It came about when I attended a community-building workshop the Foundation for Community Encouragement sponsored.

Fifty-three people gathered in a conference room and spent three days together with no agenda other than to build ourselves into a community. At the end of those three days, I felt connected to everyone in that room in a way I had never felt before in my thirty-three years. This was a remarkably diverse group. We had strong differences of opinion on everything—religion, politics, and even the simple meanings of words. With the help of our facilitators, though, we managed to discover our oneness. It was a unity that transcended all the particulars of our religious and intellectual constructs. I felt connections with people in the room with whom I had disagreed rather strongly. It was as though we had learned to look at each other with new eyes. With those new eyes, I could see beyond my doubts and the intellectual rigidity of my fixed religious and cultural position and into the eyes of other struggling human beings who were just like me. It wasn't that I had lost my hard-earned religious ideas and moral principles. I still had them, but my relationship to them was different. I no longer had to cling to them so tightly to define myself in the world.

As I processed this experience in the following days, I realized I had spiritually changed in some incomprehensible way. I felt as if I had broken through another boundary, and I was trying to step over another threshold. As I let the profundity of the event settle into my life, Marla's words eventually returned to me. "Only when you are capable of doubting your doubts will you find true freedom and take the next step on your spiritual journey." This mystical community experience did not exactly make me doubt my doubts, but it did lead me to carry them a little less close to my vest. This freed me to be with and experience other people in a more compassionate way.

Religious language helped me to frame this experience also. What happened in that workshop was actually a type of mystical experience. For the first time in my life, it struck me on some deep, existential level that everyone in that room was a child of God. Everyone had something of the divine, and that included me. Christ presented himself to me through everyone in that room, whether or not each particular person self-identified as a Christian. In God's eyes each was already whole and holy and could re-present Christ to me. I just needed to awaken to that realization.

As a result of this experience of community and others, I gradually became better able to let go of some of my defensiveness and intellectual snobbery. I could actually be with people who were in different religious and spiritual places than me. I had moved into another place in my spiritual development.

There have been remarkable people through the ages who have been able to maintain the type of vision I had during those few days during and after the community-building experience. Those people were able to continually see the interconnectedness of all human beings, living creatures, and even inanimate matter in a way that shaped their very characters. These were those rare individuals who saw the great mystery that is life, and rather than escape it, they sought to penetrate ever deeper into it. They became mystics. This is in contrast to the prevailing way of being wherein people survive by separating and categorizing things and people in this spatial and temporal biological existence.

Something finally helped me make sense of all the things that had happened to me over this span of many years. I realized my faith had changed in rather dramatic ways as I had negotiated through these experiences. As I processed these changes in my life, I began to see similar development in others, and I began to notice there are rather distinct ways individuals think and process as their faith develops. While conceding that all individuals have unique spiritual journeys, there did seem to be a discernable pattern in faith development. I concluded that most people who take the steps courageous faith requires seem to go through these phases or stages:

- Adopted Faith
- Individuating Faith
- Holistic Faith

The first stage of faith development is "Adopted Faith." This stage characterizes the majority of mainstream churchgoers and "true believers," at least in Western society. It's similar in other cultures and religions in the sense that people adopt the basic beliefs and tenets of the established, institutional religions and cling to them rather vociferously. These people are essentially attached to the forms rather than the substance of their religions. They have generally turned to religion for clear-cut answers, and they are usually legalistic, dogmatic, and parochial in their thinking and ways of speaking. Religion is a way for them to escape mystery as opposed to a way of approaching it. Therefore, even if they are relatively well educated, which many of them are, they usually fail to apply critical thinking in matters of faith. A significant number have undergone dramatic conversions from unstructured lives before they adopted religious faith. As such, they get very upset when someone plays fast and loose with the rules that define the institution because the institution helps define them as people. They consciously or subconsciously resist situations that invite critical reflection about the beliefs and values of the institutional religion that governs them. They do not understand people who have moved to Individuating or Holistic Faith, and generally they regard them as people who have lost their faith or become backsliders. They fail to see value in growing beyond Adopted Faith, and sometimes they even try to prevent others from moving on and furthering their faith developments into Individuating or Holistic Faith. They discourage honest questions and doubts rather than acknowledging them as a necessary part of faith development. People at this stage are very reliant on interpersonal relationships with others in the religious institution in order to foster belonging. Generally they are unlikely to venture far from groupthink. The mores and values of the tradition govern them, so they are generally good people and hard workers with good values who add strength to their institutions. There are people at the Adopted Faith stage in all faith traditions. However, in their dogmatic extremes, they are also the ones that insist they know better than anyone else what constitutes proper faith development and spiritual formation.

The next stage is Individuating Faith. These are people who have internalized many of the principles of their Adopted Faith. They are self-governing individuals who might not claim allegiances to any particular religious institution. They are scientific and submit all their beliefs to the crucible of logical scrutiny. They might self-identify as atheists or agnostics. However, this does not necessarily mean they disparage spirituality. Often they are people of enormous spiritual depth and power precisely *because* of the unflinching ways they submit their beliefs to logic and rational investigation. They might be individualistic, but they are often deeply committed to social and humanitarian causes. They are active truth seekers and usually have high moral standards. Does that sound familiar to you? Perhaps it does. Generally people who have evolved at least as far as this stage read books such as this. They are religious seekers but are not always content with the packaged answers religious institutions offer. Prodded into further investigation by their realizations that the human religious experience is much too colorful and varied to be explained by any one-size-fits-all spirituality, their restlessness directs them into a more reflective place. Such a place is more intellectualizing perhaps, but also more rational and circumspect. These people take matters of faith and spirituality so seriously they are willing to accept the pain involved in breaking their vows or sacrificing their allegiances to the accepted religions of their cultures or their families. Rather than isolate matters of religion and faith from their reason and intellect, these people have taken the courageous steps necessary to bring their spiritual lives out into the light of day. Therefore, they can begin to lead lives of integrity and wholeness.

If a person persists in his or her search for integrity and wholeness, that person might finally arrive at what I call Holistic Faith. Holistic, whole, and holy sharing the same etymological root (see chapter 8.) People who have reached the stage of Holistic Faith have come to embrace life in its entirety as a whole. They see the oneness and the interconnectedness of all human beings, living creatures, and even inanimate matter in a way that shapes their very characters. This is in contrast to the prevailing way of being where people survive by separating and categorizing things and people in this spatial and temporal biological existence. These are rare individuals who see the great mystery that is life, and rather than try to escape it, they seek to penetrate even deeper into it. They are the mystics. This means they embrace mystery whether they are the contemplatives of Christianity, the Sufis of Islam, Zen Buddhists, or the mystical arms of some other religion. They palpably recognize a connectedness underlying a material universe of discrete objects. They are spiritual bridge builders. They are always yearning for the experience of oneness with others and never categorizing or dividing people because of religious beliefs or intellectual constructs. While deeply respectful of scriptures and traditions, they have so internalized the essential truth of the sacred writings that these scriptures no longer function as intervening filters separating them from others of differing beliefs. Through direct experience of the oneness at the heart of the universe, they can reinterpret and revive the symbols and texts that have gone stale for those still at the

Adopted Faith stage. Those of Holistic Faith might appear to have come back to believe many of the things they formerly believed in Adopted Faith. Often, though, they are feared, dismissed, or even reviled because they believe with a freedom that scares the hell out of those still stuck at the Adopted Faith stage.

Looking back at that coming-of-age experience I had during my college years, I was finally able to accept my doubts as a trustworthy, dependable way of dealing with the great questions of God and religious life. This was my transition from Adopted Faith to Individuating Faith. The profound, life-altering community-building experience was the time in my faith journey when I began the move from Individuating Faith into Holistic Faith. I was not able to maintain the intensity of that mystical experience of Holistic Faith for long, but while I was there I learned what it was like. Now I am able to feel some kinship with those throughout history who have had similar experiences. There was also a residual effect of that brief experience that opened me up in ways I still do not fully understand. I've contemplated it many times and spent an enormous amount of time and energy trying to come to grips with it. It's still impossible to even begin to explain, and it remains rather mysterious. I do think, though, that it made me into a more loving, compassionate human being. I find I am now better able to be with and experience others in different spiritual places. I see them in new light and feel more compassion for them and the perspectives to which some cling. These life experiences have convinced me it is supremely important to learn about these stages of faith development and to teach them to others in order to make progress toward a better understanding of one another. This is essential if the world is ever going to become a more peaceful place.

Let me conclude this topic by reiterating that not everyone is in the same spiritual place. Everyone is on a spiritual journey, and hopefully that journey assists each person in feeling more at home in the universe and more compassionate toward fellow travelers on this tiny planet. Universalism has been helpful to me because it has allowed me to love others more wholeheartedly and feel less of a need to heal them or convert them to my way of thinking. Though the ways of God still remain very much a mystery to me, I have much more peace on my own spiritual journey because I am secure in the knowledge that God works in and through us all.

* * *

ten

The Apostle Paul—Paradigm of Adopted Faith

Paul of Tarsus, known as the Apostle Paul, arguably has had a greater influence on the shape of Western civilization than any other human being. I base this little piece of conjecture on two facts. First, Paul or Pauline writers wrote two-thirds of the New Testament (the defining text of Christianity). Scholars generally agree that Paul's letters were the first New Testament writings, and he provided us with the first written account of what it is to be a Christian and what was expected of members of the Christian community. Secondly, despite its recent decline in developed nations, Christianity remains the largest religion in the world. It claims about one-third of the world's population. Whether or not my conjecture is accurate, it is nonetheless generally agreed that Christianity today would be vastly different without Paul's influence. Some even question whether Christianity would exist at all.

Paul was a Hellenistic Jew, a Roman citizen, and a trained Pharisee. According to his own testimony, Paul violently persecuted the early Christians. These people were known as followers of "The Way." Then Paul underwent a dramatic conversion experience on the road to Damascus sometime around AD 33 to 36. There is no record of him ever knowing Jesus personally before the cruci-fixion. Little is known about his life from the time of his conversion until fourteen years later when he began his missionary work. In the late forties and all through the fifties, Paul traveled extensively throughout the northeastern Mediterranean. On these missionary journeys, usually with a companion, he preached and taught about a new relationship between God and humanity based on a theol-ogy of atonement. Paul taught that Christians were redeemed from their sins against the laws of God as outlined in the Torah by Jesus's death and resurrection. A person who accepted this doctrine mys-tically shared in Jesus's death, his victory over it, and, therefore, eternal life. He also thought Gentiles, or non-Jews, could benefit from this new relationship he called justification.

Paul made three missionary journeys. This culminated in his arrest and extradition to Rome where, according to tradition, he was beheaded. The early church recognized the importance of his letters in shaping the morals and practices of the Christian commu-nity and preserved them. Early church fathers quoted these letters as early as 96 AD. They were generally accepted as part of the bibli-cal canon by the middle of the third century.

Paul seemed to be the best historical figure to illustrate Adopted Faith. His life-changing experience on the road to Damascus is prototypical for the conversion experience by which many enter Adopted Faith. The terms "Pauline conversion" or "Damascus Road experience" are synonyms for the sudden, dramatic changes that occur in people's lives who make 180-degree turns in their moral and spiritual directions. Here is the description of Saul's conver-sion (Paul was known as Saul at this time in his life) as described in the book of Acts.

"Now as he was going along and approaching Damascus, suddenly a light from heaven flashed around him. He fell to the ground and heard a voice saying to him, 'Saul, Saul, why do you persecute me?' He asked, 'Who are you, Lord?' The reply came, 'I am Jesus, whom you are persecuting. But get up and enter the city, and you will be told what you are to do.' The men who were traveling with him stood speechless because they heard the voice but saw no one. Saul got up from the ground, and though his eyes were open, he could see nothing; so they led him by the hand and brought him into Damascus. For three days he was without sight, and neither ate nor drank."[7]

In retrospect Paul recognized the folly of his mind-set before his conversion. Here is his description of the state of his life prior to the Damascus Road. "[I was a] Hebrew born of Hebrews, as to the law, a Pharisee, as to righteousness under the law, blameless."[8] At that stage he was an up-and-coming representative of the temple in Jerusalem. He was likely consumed with advancement in his legal career. After his conversion, though, he immediately knew what his true nature had been, and he immediately recognized the evil of his previous ways. In the words of John Pollock, a modern biographer of Paul, Paul "had been mentally and spiritually hostile to God, though honoring him by mouth; he had been busy in evil, though punctilious in religious rites; he had been altogether estranged, fit for nothing but to crawl away as far as he could from the blinding light that was God."[AA]

People at this stage of faith development adopt a set of beliefs with strict interpretations of scripture and doctrine. Conformity to an established norm is their ideal and they exhibit little tolerance for those who attempt to color outside the lines of orthodoxy. As

---

7   Acts 9:3–9.
8   Phil. 3:5–6

one of the founders of the fledgling Christianity, Paul was especially sensitive to any deviation from what he saw as the true faith. His letters indicate he was meticulous over issues of doctrinal interpretation. He expected his code of belief to be adopted in the communities he established, and he brooked little or no dissent among the ranks of his followers. Interestingly, being "adopted" by God was one of Paul's favorite metaphors, and he and the Pauline community that came after him used it often.[9]

The message of Paul's writing, especially during the early years of his public ministry, reveals someone highly focused on laying out the justifications for this strict code of religious and community practice he was establishing for the new churches. He obsessed over issues of inclusivity and exclusivity as he sought to reconcile with some measure of integrity devotees to Jesus from both the Jewish and Gentile communities. Viewed from a twenty-first-century perspective, Paul's attitudes seem quaint and anachronistic. Many passages suggest a second-class status for women—although the majority of these passages come from letters where Paul's authorship is doubted. Most scholars would agree, given the social and legal context in which he was writing, Paul was radically inclusive—at least for Gentiles, women, and slaves. He wrote, "there is no longer Jew or Greek, slave or free, male or female, all of you are one in Christ Jesus."[10] With this he wanted to put an end, at least within the church, to the social and economic divisions common in that societal era.

If we can deduce anything about Paul's character from his extant writings, foremost would be his tenacity in maintaining his convictions once formed. The zealousness with which he hammered home the details of the faith he espoused eclipsed even the

---

9 See Gal. 4:5, Rom. 8:15, and Eph. 1:5.
10 Gal. 3:28.

zeal with which he persecuted Christians before his conversion. He spilled much ink in setting his followers straight when he felt they erred. He was obviously an intense, driven man—fervent to the point of obstinacy. This is also typical of people at the Adopted Faith stage. They are known to become quite upset if anyone tries to make any changes in the accepted way of doing things. There is psychological justification for this. Since the "truth" came to them in a particular way, and it had dramatic effects in liberating them from their chaotic lives before Adopted Faith, they are wary and even threatened when anyone tries to change the words, symbols, or literary shape of the community's practices that transmit and preserve that truth.

When Paul's writings are read literally and legalistically as a prescription for community in all places at all times, he comes across as very much prototypical of Adopted Faith. He gave clear-cut, dogmatic criteria for inclusion in the church community. The principles of relationship and conduct he outlined sometimes hearkened back to the spirit rather than the letter of Jewish law. However, once these principles were institutionalized, they quickly became criteria for defining an in-group and an out-group in typical Adopted Faith style. Paul defined a religious community that obviously had enormous appeal to many people in a chaotic society. The church he founded went viral, in a sense, over the next three hundred years to become not only legally recognized but the dominant religion of the Western world.

This characterization is not meant to either glorify or vilify Paul and his writings. It is descriptive of the dynamic which Paul utilized to insure the churches he started took shape as he envisioned. The Christian church that Paul was so influential in founding and shaping largely epitomizes the stage of Adopted Faith on an orgazational level. As James Fowler, another author who has written extensively on spiritual growth and development, said, "In many ways religious institutions work best if they are peopled with a majority of committed folk best described by [this stage.]"[BB] With Adopted Faith types, authority is generally entrusted to a source outside themselves, their reason, and their consciousness. Paul filled this need for a voice of authority. His writings to the scattered communities of the first century church form a nexus which many church communities today use as a template in determining how church members are to understand God, Christ, and be in relationship to one another.

Paul has great appeal to many people at the Adopted Faith level of spiritual development. By buying into Paul's neat framing of community belief and conduct, they have a convenient way to escape what Scott Peck called "the mystery of uncertainty in the ever moving and expanding unknown."[CC] This is quite characteristic of those in Adopted Faith or in Peck's somewhat parallel stage II spiritual growth. Over a period of two thousand years, therefore, instead of becoming a community open to new, imaginative, and expanding possibilities in human relations, as the church was originally, the church has self selected to some extent a community of those who choose the stagnation of formulations, prescribed methods, and doctrines. This way of being in community inevitably spells out a way of life less imaginative, creative, and dynamic and more preoccupied with enforcing doctrinal norms and escaping the fear of uncertainty.

My intention is not to vilify Paul, nor is my categorization of the Christian church as largely an Adopted Faith organization meant to denigrate it. Christianity has contributed much of enormous value to the world. It preserved civilization and much great literature and knowledge through the Dark Ages. It inspired so much exquisite music, art, and architecture. The system of higher education can trace its roots to the monastic communities of the Christian church. The first systems of health care and care for orphans and other disadvantaged people originated within it. Many basic values of caring and compassion that form the basis of our culture owe much to the preserving influence of the Christian Church. Therefore, Adopted Faith institutions, just like Adopted Faith people, can be powerful forces for good in the world.

Churches are generally places of interpersonal warmth and meaning for people at both the Adopted and Holistic Faith stages. Those in Adopted Faith largely accept the images and symbols of conventional faith unreflectively. Still, they can experience the transcendent in and through church liturgy and ritual. Those with holistic faith likely interpret these things symbolically and metaphorically, and they derive meaning and even transcendence from that way of understanding them. It's the Individuating Faith types that generally can't find a home in the church. This has been and continues to be the great challenge for the institutional church. True, people can and do progress from Adopted Faith to Holistic Faith without going into full rebellion or becoming atheists. However, when the church assumes a defensive posture with someone struggling with legitimate questions and doubts, this posture sends the wrong message to those entering Individuating Faith. A person at the verge of Individuating Faith is endeavoring to maintain the integrity of their inner life and worldview. When the church negates or vilifies their doubts and questions, it often pushes them away. People often need time, space, and a proper supportive environment to work through their doubts. They need encouragement to embrace and cherish their doubts as a necessary part of achieving healthy spirituality.

Doubts are also an essential part of the oversight process of the church (or any institution). Doubts help people prevent unsavory and disreputable types from invading and corrupting. This is a challenge the church has historically avoided rather than face. This discouragement of doubt and healthy skepticism has led to a consistent pattern of the church driving growing people out of its community. This refusal of the church to honor healthy skepticism and doubt makes many in Individuative Faith leave and stay away. Individuative faith types are likely to reason that its better to maintain integrity and stay in a spiritual place of perpetual resistance rather than return to a religion or an institution where their views are not welcomed or appreciated. Reacting to the intransigence of an Adopted Faith church, Individuating Faith types may become just as dogmatic in their skepticism.

Paul's writings are the epitomy of Adopted Faith spirituality. The clear-cut, black-and-white, either/or mind-set is evident in virtually all his theses. There are no half measures. He is self-assured to the point of arrogance in what he wrote. As he said to the Galatians, "I am astonished that you are so quickly deserting the one who called you in the grace of Christ and are turning to a different gospel—not that there is another gospel." "If anyone proclaims to you a gospel contrary to what you received [the one I have given you], let that one be accursed."[11]

Another way Paul typifies adopted faith is the fastidiousness with which he defined the in-group and out-group. This is a timeless way of creating a provincial, tight-knit community. Rigid rules are set, and a charismatic, authoritarian leader defines unequivocal boundaries and vilifies those who think outside the defined conventions. The world is divided into "believers" and "unbelievers," "saved" and "unsaved," or some other designation, and those outside the defined boundaries need to be fixed or converted before they are worthy of consideration. This served the Christian community well when they were an underground, persecuted minority. Whether this method has been in the best interest of the church since it achieved majority standing in most Western civilizations is much more debatable.

---

11 Gal. 1:6-8.

There is a place for Adopted Faith in the spiritual growth and development of everyone. One could no more skip over Adopted Faith than one could omit one of the psychosocial stages of Erik Erikson or do without the basics in Maslow's hierarchy of needs before jumping straight into self-actualization. Each stage requires learning a particular way of processing experiences and information, learning that is essential for a developing human spirit. Grace and goodness come in full measure in each stage according to the developing person's needs. There are people with gifts and talents the world needs at all stages of faith development. The essential problem derives when large institutions fail to see value in growing beyond Adopted Faith.

There is so much more potential in the human spirit. When Paul becomes the defining paradigm for humanity's greatest spiritual aspirations, which is true in some circles, the ability to achieve the full potential of the individual or of the community is truncated. A sensitive yet critical reader of Paul's works will see that even Paul recognized the limitations of his approach. He wrote to the Corinthians, "And so, brothers and sisters, I could not speak to you as spiritual people, but rather as people of the flesh, as infants in Christ. I fed you with milk, not solid food, for you were not ready for solid food. Even now you are still not ready."[12]

Some of the writings of the mature Paul offer glimpses of a person who was beginning to embrace a more holistic, universal vision. His thesis on love from the book of Corinthians is perhaps one of the best ever written on the subject. They convey a beautiful, mystical message for the full flowering of human potential and community. It sounds remarkably like someone in the Holistic Faith stage. In the spirit of giving Paul a fair and balanced reading, I will close this chapter with his words.

---

12 I Cor. 3:1–2.

"If I speak in the tongues of mortals and of angels, but do not have love, I am a noisy gong or a clanging cymbal. And if I have prophetic powers, and understand all mysteries and all knowledge, and if I have all faith, so as to remove mountains, but do not have love, I am nothing. If I give away all my possessions, and if I hand over my body so that I may boast, but do not have love, I gain nothing. Love is patient; love is kind; love is not envious or boastful or arrogant or rude. It does not insist on its own way; it is not irritable or resentful; it does not rejoice in wrongdoing, but rejoices in the truth. It bears all things, believes all things, hopes all things, endures all things. Love never ends. But as for prophecies, they will come to an end; as for tongues, they will cease; as for knowledge, it will come to an end. For we know only in part, and we prophesy only in part; but when the complete comes, the partial will come to an end. When I was a child, I spoke like a child, I thought like a child, I reasoned like a child; when I became an adult, I put an end to childish ways. For now we see in a mirror, dimly, but then we will see face to face. Now I know only in part; then I will know fully, even as I have been fully known. And now faith, hope, and love abide, these three; and the greatest of these is love."[13]

* * *

---

13 I Cor. 13:1–13.

eleven

Bertrand Russell—Paradigm of Individuating Faith

"There is a marvelous anecdote from the occasion of Bertrand Russell's ninetieth birthday that best serves to summarize his attitude toward God and religion. A London lady sat next to him at this party, and over the soup she suggested to him that he was not only the world's most famous atheist but, by this time, very probably the world's oldest atheist. 'What will you do, Bertie, if it turns out you're wrong?' she asked. 'I mean, what if—uh—when the time comes, you should meet Him? What will you say?' Russell was delighted with the question. His bright, birdlike eyes grew even brighter as he contemplated this possible future dialogue, and then he pointed a finger upward and cried, 'Why, I should say, "God, you gave us insufficient evidence."'"[DD]

This is a very good summary of the religious perspective of the philosopher Bertrand Russell (1870–1972). As a philosopher Russell was interested in what he could know for certain. His passion for certainty in knowledge made him one of the foremost philosophers of the twentieth century and perhaps the greatest logical thinker since Aristotle. He said two things led him to study philosophy—this desire for certain knowledge and a desire to find some satisfaction for religious impulses. These religious impulses found no locus in traditional Christianity. Russell had rejected all the tenets of his puritan upbringing by eighteen after subjecting them to rigorous logical analysis. His religious yearnings found a home in the logical certainty of mathematics. He had an almost mystical attraction to mathematics and said it possessed not only truth but supreme beauty. During his teen years, he became sullen and depressed. Later he said only his desire to know more mathematics saved him from suicide.[EE]

He made major contributions in the fields of philosophy and mathematics in the early 1900s before turning to social, political, and educational issues. His views were liberal and progressive. He supported antiwar efforts, birth control, women's rights, and the rights of homosexuals before such perspectives were ever discussed in mainstream media. He had an astounding amount of physical and mental energy, was a prolific writer and commentator, and lived to be ninety-seven. He was politically active up until the day of his death. These attributes combined with his incredibly quick mind and clever wit and made him the nightmare of every conservative pundit. He was the last public sage.

Russell is perhaps history's best example of Individuating Faith. No public figure before or since who openly professed to be atheistic has been so influential or has commanded such respect. By living long enough to see so many of his radical ideas become reality, he best exemplifies how important sound reasoning and a skeptical eye are in dealing with the complex and sometimes overwhelming issues that confront human beings. Unlike so many cynical skeptics who have gained public hearing in today's media, Russell taught how to articulate a skeptical perspective forcefully and passionately while still retaining enough humor and self-effacement to attract and remain engaged with a wide audience. He composed a life of fervent convictions and was jailed on several occasions for his antiwar and antinuclear efforts. Yet he still retained his inquisitiveness and humility. Never resting on his conclusions, he was always taking in new information. Thus he managed to change his viewpoint from time to time. These attributes make him a noteworthy example of Individuating Faith. There is much in his character and life worth emulating despite occasional inconsistencies and sometimes tragic faults.

People with Individuating Faith are skeptical and individual in how they apprehend religious and spiritual ideas. They place most of their trust in logic and the scientific method and look with suspicion on anything not objectively verifiable. Often they self-identify as atheists or agnostics. It might seem odd to think of atheists and agnostics as more spiritually developed than those in Adopted Faith (those who have submitted themselves to governance of a formal religion or institution), but those in Individuating Faith are more advanced in the grounding of their spirituality. They are more self-aware, have stood outside the conventions of traditional religious faith, and have been thoughtful and reflective about what they are being asked to believe.

The basic difference between Adopted Faith and Individuating Faith usually lies in where the members of either group locate the authority that governs their lives. Adopted Faith types usually locate authority in some source external to themselves such as the church, the Bible, or a transcendent God. Individuating Faith types, however, are self-governing. They have internalized many of the principles of civil society that govern those in Adopted Faith, and they listen to the dictates of their own consciences. (Moreover the values and principles they have adopted through rational processes have formed those consciences.) Consequently they see the codes and precepts of religious institutions as rigid and legalistic.

Questioning the givens in conventional religion is necessary to grow and develop as spiritual beings. Why? Human beings are endowed with the capacity for reason and the use of logic. This capacity has expanded the knowledge of the physical world so dramatically by its application through the scientific method. Therefore, the fruits of reason and logic are everywhere. To withhold the use of reason in understanding ourselves and our spiritual nature would go against everything we know of progress. Abandoning the innate sense of curiosity would leave humankind infantile. If there is validity to the spiritual dimension of life, then to some extent it must stand up to critical questioning. Without being able to subject spiritual understandings to rational processes, people would forever be at the mercy of every religious charlatan to come along.

Whether it is bringing forth a new marvel on the artist's canvas, on the writer's page, or in the scientist's laboratory, any creative process demands what John Keats called negative capability. Anyone involved in bringing something new into the world must be capable of being uncertain for a time and making room for doubt and mystery. That person must let go of the familiar and welcome the strange and new. This is especially true when it comes to our creation as new spiritual beings. To become a new person with new and more enlightened understandings, that person must make room for new possibilities, and that involves negative capability—looking at the other side of the great questions of life and being receptive to the possibility that the answers culture and tradition have provided are not always the whole picture.

By eighteen Russell had examined and discarded most Christian beliefs. In 1927 he summarized his views in an influential lecture called "Why I Am Not a Christian." In this lecture, later published in a book, Russell took all the rational and moral arguments advanced throughout history to justify Christianity and systematically demolished them all. In doing so Russell stated both sides of the issue, and he gave a remarkably fair hearing to the prevailing view before refuting it. For example, he examined the first cause argument for the existence of God. This theory maintains that everything in this world has a cause, and if one goes back in the chain of causes further and further, he or she must come to a first cause—God. His argument against this was who made God? Russell maintained there was no reason to suppose the world had to have any beginning at all, and the idea that things have to have beginnings was really due to a poverty of imagination.

So Russell confirmed himself as an agnostic or atheist for the remainder of his life. (He used both terms to describe himself on different occasions.) However, he never lost his sense of humor and always welcomed dialogue about religion. For instance, take the story about when Russell was jailed after participating in an illegal peace protest. His jailer asked him about his religion. Russell replied "agnostic" and spelled it for him. The jailer shook his head and said, "There's many different religions, but I suppose we all worship the same God." Russell commented that the remark cheered him for weeks. Perhaps the remark, obviously made from a position of ignorance on the jailer's part, reminded Russell that his was a faith stance also. He could no more prove the nonexistence of God than his jailer could prove God's existence. In some sort of paradoxical way, therefore, everyone does worship the same God—the one who cannot be proved one way or the other.

Russell was never flippant in his views. Like many who consider themselves atheists, he took the question of the existence of God seriously. Russell, like any sincere atheist, was someone who showed courage in dismissing the word and even the concept of God as mere idols of traditional religion. He took the religious question quite seriously, yet he never lost his sense of himself as a mere subject in his objective philosophical quest for answers about life's ultimate meaning.

Many who progress to Individuating Faith (seekers, skeptics, agnostics, and atheists) will not subsequently make the leap to Holistic Faith. The mystical, communal sense of the universe's "oneness" is beyond comprehension for many, and the trustworthiness of the skeptical posture is exactly the point for the person at this stage of faith development. Religious experiences, intuition, mysticism, and anything beyond empirical data, factual construction, and scientific measurement is not to be trusted and should, therefore, be rejected. Alfred Jules Ayer, credited with carrying on Russell's work, expressed the sentiment well.

> "We conclude, therefore, that the argument from religious experience is altogether fallacious. The fact that people have religious experiences is interesting from the psychological point of view, but it does not in any way imply that there is such a thing as religious knowledge, any more than our having moral experiences implies that there is such a thing as moral knowledge. The theist, like the moralist, may believe that his experiences are cognitive experiences, but, unless he can formulate his 'knowledge' in propositions that are empirically verifiable, we may be sure that he is deceiving himself. It follows that these philosophers who fill their books with assertions that they intuitively 'know' this or that moral or religious 'truth' are merely providing material for the psycho-analyst. For no act of intuition can be said to reveal a truth about any matter of fact unless it issues in verifiable propositions."[FF]

While I have great respect and even empathy for the sincere skeptic, I am also keenly aware there is a dimension of reality that is and will undoubtedly remain in the realm of ambiguity and mystery. I have had religious experiences as many others have as well, and I can no more explain them than I can explain the beauty of a flower. I know, though, the experiences were real. It's the same way I know the love I feel toward my family and they feel toward me is real. I would even say people can gain a measure of truth from religious experience. This includes that mystical feeling of oneness with others often felt in community. That profound truth can't be boiled down to verifiable fact. This type of truth is qualitatively different from what anyone can gain from factual knowledge. It is of a totally different order.

Russell himself had a mystical experience at twenty-eight, and this changed his whole life. He was completely overcome while watching the intense suffering of a friend. This is what he wrote about that experience.

"Suddenly the ground seemed to give way beneath me, and I found myself in quite another region. Within five minutes I went through some such reflections as the following: the loneliness of the human soul is unendurable; nothing can penetrate it except the highest intensity of the sort of love that religious teachers have preached; whatever does not spring from this motive is harmful, or at best useless, it follows that war is wrong...that the use of force is to be deprecated, and that in human relations one should penetrate to the core of loneliness in each person and speak to that...

At the end of those five minutes, I had become a completely different person. For a time, a sort of mystic illumination possessed me. I felt that I knew the inmost thoughts of everybody that I met in the street, and though this was, no doubt, a delusion, I did in actual fact find myself in far closer touch than previously with all my friends, and many of my acquaintances. Having been an imperialist I became during those five minutes a...pacifist. Having for years cared only for exactness and analysis, I found myself filled with semimystical feelings about beauty, with an intense interest in children, and with a desire almost as profound as that of the Buddha to find some philosophy which should make human life endurable."GG

From all indication Russell underwent a change of character as a result of this experience. From that day forward, he changed his political views and became a devoted pacifist. He remained so until his death. He also became quite interested in children, and he devoted much of his time and energy to educational psychology and research. He referred back to this mystical experience frequently as a turning point in his life, yet he never assigned any religious interpretation to it. He did, therefore, remain true to his logical way of processing most everything. That is to say, just because he could not give a valid scientific explanation for the experience, it was no reason to assign it to some sort of supernatural or divine intervention. This experience obviously profoundly moved Russell to become a more caring and compassionate person. A religious person would automatically be inclined to think of it in terms of a divine act. For a secular person such as Russell, though, it could remain profound, powerful, and mysterious without having to carry any religious labeling.

Going back to the story of the elderly Russell being asked to imagine an encounter with God, it seems that even this experience, powerful though it was, counted as insufficient evidence for Russell's belief in God, according to his way of thinking and processing the mystery of life. Still, he remained delighted with life for all his ninety-seven remarkable years. He was a man of enormous spirit, compassion, and prophetic voice. (Although, if alive, he would likely resist some of those descriptive terms.) His life proved how passionate skepticism can lead to a life of remarkable courage and outstanding achievement. He validated skepticism and individuality as vital parts of the process of becoming spiritually whole.

* * *

twelve

Gandhi—Paradigm of Holistic Faith

Einstein had this to say about Gandhi: "Generations to come will scarce believe that such a one as this ever in flesh and blood walked upon this earth."[HH]

Gandhi attracted many close followers during his lifetime, and many ashrams (religious communes) grew up around him as he moved about. Men, women, and children from all backgrounds and nationalities came to meet him and be utterly and completely drawn into lives of devotion and service. One of the very first people to come under Gandhi's spell was Jawaharlal Nehru—the man who would become independent India's first prime minister. Nehru came from a very cultured, wealthy Hindu family, and he was educated at great expense in Cambridge, England. Nehru gave up the lavish way of life he had acquired under British influence, and he poured his money, time, and talent into Gandhi's movement for India's independence. Nehru's father, a wealthy, powerful lawyer, went to Gandhi to beg for his son's return. "You have taken our only son," his father said to Gandhi. "Give him back to us, and I will put my wealth at the disposal of your campaign." Gandhi only shook his head and said, "Not only do I want your son, I want you, and your wife, and your daughters, and the rest of your family too." Gandhi ended up getting them all, beginning with the father.[II]

Just to meet Gandhi was to risk being enchanted and having one's whole life changed into that of a hero. Gandhi demanded devotion to the point of death, and he got it. Even his enemies fell under the spell of his indomitable spirit and personality. "Don't go near Gandhi," new British administrators were cautioned as they came ashore in India. "Don't go near Gandhi; he'll get you."[JJ]

Mohandas Gandhi was such a tiny, ordinary man. As a child he was painfully shy and afraid of the dark. He grew up a less-than-average student, and he failed in multiple careers before studying law and then failing at that. How did he manage to transform himself into the spiritual giant who led his people to fight and win their independence from the greatest, most far-flung empire the world had ever known?

Gandhi credited an incident in South Africa as the creative moment that completely changed his life. He was thrown from a train because of his refusal to give up the first-class seat for which he had a rightful ticket. As he sat in a cold, unlit railroad station all night, he pondered humanity's inhumanity and the persecution he and others were forced to endure because of differences in skin color and religious beliefs. He resolved then and there to never yield to force and to never use violence in championing a cause.

While in South Africa, Gandhi began to enjoy some measure of success as an arbitrator, but the financial rewards gave him no satisfaction. He began to devote himself to community service, and the joy he experienced in selfless service to others began to take hold of his entire being. The more he simplified his life, the more freedom and energy he had to plunge into other acts of service, and his desire to live for others grew ever stronger. He began living life as an experiment, and his own inner life became his laboratory. He had read much about truth and happiness, but he found little use for theories and abstractions. He wanted to know how to live for more than money, prestige, and pleasure—those things the world values—and he was willing to submit his entire character and deepest convictions in this quest. He studied other religious faiths, but he finally found what he was looking for in his own spiritual tradition—specifically in Hindu epic of the *Bhagavad Gita*. The conversations between Krishna, the lord of love, and Arjuna, the warrior, on the battlefield became Gandhi's instruction book in fighting the battles within his own heart. Our desires bring us into conflict in the world, Gandhi learned from Krishna. So Gandhi began to do battle against the forces of darkness and separation within himself. He simultaneously engaged the British authorities in South Africa in seeking civil rights for his people.

For Gandhi, the fiercest and most dangerous war *was* the one in his own consciousness. He could not declare nonviolence and peace to the world until he found it in himself. By meditating on the *Gita* day and night, Gandhi became a living testimonial to the transformation described in its pages. Gandhi said, "The Gita has been a mother to me ever since I became first acquainted with it. I turn to it for guidance in every difficulty, and the desired guidance has always been forthcoming. But you must approach Mother Gita in all reverence, if you would benefit by her ministrations. One who rests his head on her peace-giving lap never experiences disappointment but enjoys bliss in perfection. This spiritual mother gives her devotee fresh knowledge, hope and power every moment of his life."[KK]

Most know the rest of his story. Gandhi developed a theory of civil disobedience that he described using Sanskrit terms—satyagraha (truth force) and ahimsa (nonviolence to all living things). Under the theory Gandhi developed, the goal was not to forget that the oppressed and oppressor were one. The aim was not to vanquish the opponent but to win the enemy over by the force of love and make that enemy an ally in the struggle for truth and justice. Gandhi put these principles to the test in South Africa, and his modest successes there enabled him to enter the world stage as the leader of India's struggle for independence from Britain.

Many well known figures could have been used to illustrate Holistic Faith. However the life of Gandhi presents two rather distinct advantages. First, he wrote prolifically. Therefore we know a lot about how his thought and his inner life developed. Second, he came to attention after the advent of global mass communication. As his life played out on the world's stage he was quite effective in sharing his thoughts and reflections on events in real time even as he helped to shape them. His spiritual life became a public drama in ways that had not happened before nor perhaps since. His life presents a rather unique opportunity as a model for Holistic Faith. I say this while conceding that Gandhi had his faults. He admitted to and dealt with some, and others he never seemed to come to grips with. What I have presented thus far is Gandhi the legend— the sanitized, mythic version who lives in the ideal part of our collective mind. Gandhi the man is a much more complex study. For all attempts to canonize him as a saint, his private life was too public. He neglected and humiliated his wife and insisted she follow all his austere ways. At thirty-six he unilaterally declared himself celibate and tested himself by sleeping beside the young women of his ashrams. He might have demonstrated power over his baser nature, but never took into account the psychological and emotional effects this might have had on those young women. He also sought to impose his ways on his children, and he gave them little room to be their own people. He was not the ideal family man. He also brooked no challenge to his authority in his ashrams or in the movement for independence that took shape around him. Was he perfect? No. He was a compassionate, insightful human being who became possessed by a vision that took on a life of its own. He was, though, a flawed human being. Was there some special quality to his spirituality that can speak to us today and inform and sustain our own spiritual quests? Absolutely. One of the keys to unlock that potential is to focus on how his life can instruct us toward a better understanding of this mystical stage called Holistic Faith.

To understand Holistic Faith, it's necessary to have some understanding of mysticism. Mysticism means much the same as the word "mystery." However, it is Mystery with a capital M. That is, it is not like a murder mystery where one can apply powers of reason to the collected facts and come up with a solution. This type of Mystery has a spiritual sense and will only deepen the more one tries to plumb its depths. Like love or faith, it cannot be reduced to terms completely transmissible through human language. There are mystics in every religious tradition. The kabbalah within Judaism, Sufism within Islam, and Christian mysticism within Christianity are examples. In fact, all religions began in the mystical experience—God speaking to Abraham, Moses witnessing the burning bush, the Buddha meditating under the bo tree, or Jesus fasting in the desert. Mystics come away from profound depth experiences with new awareness of the unity that underlies everything. This connectedness between all living beings and even the cosmos itself is beyond ordinary perceptive capacities, and it eclipses the usual ways of perceiving, dividing, and classifying the universe.

Both the nonreligious and religious in society often denigrate mysticism. It is, in essence, mystery and so it's easy to see why it is a difficult concept to grasp. The mystic seeks apprehension of and communion with the divine or transcendent through intuition and direct experience.

Because mystics seek to know religious truth empirically through direct experience, they rely less on established doctrine. This is why many traditionalists and institutional religions disparage the mystical path. Those who can't read beyond the tenets of their faiths and those who are grounded solely in reason look suspiciously upon mystics. Mystics can even be considered dangerous because of their tendencies toward more poetic readings of scripture. This gives them license to love beyond the normal provincial circles of the religious traditions from which they come.

Love beyond his own circles is exactly what Gandhi did. Soon after his return to India in 1915, he renounced virtually all possessions and began to live with the harijans—the untouchables. This was the real heart of Gandhi's mission. He truly lived his values. Because of this, his words carried meaning. When a well-dressed, well-fed missionary came to Gandhi and asked him how to help the poor people in the villages, Gandhi gave him an answer that challenged the very core of his being. "We must step down from our pedestals and live with them—not as outsiders, but as one of them in every way, sharing their burdens and sorrows."[LL] Just as the rich young ruler who approached Jesus, this missionary probably went away sad and unable to make such a radical renunciation. Gandhi taught by example his deep conviction that underneath everything we are all one.

His vision of oneness extended to the truth he saw in the scriptures of all the world's great religious traditions. Typical of mystics Gandhi did not think there was only one brand of truth. To him the Sermon on the Mount carried the same basic message as the *Gita*. His eclectic approach to religion puzzled many, and he was often asked what religion he claimed. He would answer, "I am a Muslim and a Hindu and a Christian and a Jew."[MM] He saw no contradiction in this statement. Unlike so many people with one-dimensional spirituality, he always thought in paradoxical terms of "both/and" rather than the exclusive "either/or."

Mystics are often quite bright and analytical but give credence to the spiritual life and to some ultimate reality beyond themselves such as God. Therefore, the scientific, skeptical Individuating Faith types eye them somewhat suspiciously. Anything beyond the human ability to analyze empirically and observe scientifically is suspect. Since mysticism is totally reliant on the subjective experience of God (or whatever the mystic calls the transcendent), the object of that experience is almost impossible to describe in language much less study in any sort of analytical way. The usual distinction between subject and object is not only difficult but impossible to make. After all, the mystic often claims union with the divine or transcendent reality. It was to a "show me" skeptic Individuating Faith type that the Buddha likely addressed his famous sermon when he said nothing but simply held forth a flower as the sum total of his great message. Any attempt to try to explain his demonstrative sermon would actually have detracted from its poetic meaning. People can only go with their experiences of the flower, and they either get the idea of beauty or they don't.

Gandhi, like all great mystics, saw divinity in all beings. Ordinary ways of thinking create a dualism for everything. This is human. This is divine. This convenient way of splitting the universe does not bind mystics. The caste system of Hinduism especially incensed Gandhi, and he lived in such a way to denounce this classification of people. He refused to enter the great temples because they were closed to the untouchables. "There is no God here," he chastened the people of India. "If God were here, everyone would have access. He is in every one of us."[NN] Because of the shame people felt upon hearing these words from Gandhi and out of the great love they had for him, these exclusionary practices began to change.

Gandhi treated every encounter as a holy one, and he sought to find God in everyone—even his enemies. He taught his followers, "If you don't find God in the next person you meet, it is a waste of time looking any further."[OO] "I cannot find God apart from humanity."[PP]

Gandhi taught nonviolence in the extreme. For Gandhi possessing anything someone else in the world needed was a form of violence too. "Ahimsa is not the crude thing it has been made to appear," he said. "Not to hurt any living thing is no doubt a part of ahimsa. But it is its least expression...It is also violated by our holding on to what the world needs."[QQ] Few are capable of the type of renunciation he lived and taught. However, we can learn from his teaching, even if incapable of living his ascetic lifestyle. On one level he did mean for his words to be taken literally. On another level, though, he was saying that to find true joy in life, one can't be attached to anything—money, possessions, or status. The moment one is attached to those things, that person becomes the objects' servant rather than the servant of others.

Later in life Gandhi reflected back on what he had accomplished. "I am an average man with less than average ability," he said. "I admit that I am not sharp intellectually. But I don't mind. There is a limit to the development of the intellect but none to that of the heart." [RR] For Gandhi developing a heart of service and compassion took him into realms of wisdom those with far superior intellects rarely access. If Gandhi's life says anything, it is that a person's level of intelligence has very little to do with what is necessary to be spiritually actualized. People can become wiser as individuals and as a community by developing emotionally. I don't think Gandhi meant for others to make development of the heart a goal alongside other goals. Emotional development only comes about as people's hearts are changed in the process of service to others. As we become part of a community of people who are striving to serve and provide acceptance and love, then this development becomes integral to the dynamic processes of being in community together.

Gandhi lived life in such a way that he claimed the hearts and minds of everyone who fell into his sphere of influence—a sphere that extended well beyond his death. "Don't go near Gandhi—he'll get you," the British government warned its new arrivals. Such is Gandhi's indomitable spirit that the same warning needs to be issued to subsequent generations. After all, his mystical spirit got Martin Luther King, Nelson Mandela, Lech Walesa, Aung San Suu Kyi, and in some mystical way, can get us too. Gandhi the mythic figure lives on in the best part of our collective vision. The way of the mystic is like that. It reaches beyond itself in time, space, and personality through some strange, mysterious means to call us toward the wholeness and oneness of true life.

* * *

thirteen

The Life Force Power of the Universe

"Religion is a story that the left brain tells the right brain."
—Jill Bolte Taylor

Dr. Jill Bolte Taylor has a rather unique story. While working as a neuroscientist in Harvard's brain research center, she had a sudden, uninvited, mystical experience. This experience came to her as the result of a stroke.

One morning in December 1996, Taylor woke up with a searing pain behind her left eye. A blood vessel had popped in the left side of her brain. Over the course of four hours, she gradually lost her ability to walk, talk, read, and write. She lost the memories of her past, and she finally lost consciousness itself. As these functions slipped away, the higher functions of her left brain were dissolving as well. This included the ability to see herself as a single entity occupying space and time and as someone with a job, relationships, and responsibilities. Her capacity to see the world with her left brain, the analytical processor of reality, came and went over those four hours. During the periods when these functions of the left brain would go off-line, she felt wonderful. Only when her rational, analytical self returned would she panic and become fearful about what was happening. While all this was going on, she vacillated between periods of complete ecstasy and moments of tremendous fearfulness. When her right side became paralyzed, her left brain said, "Oh, my gosh. I'm having a stroke!" The next moment her right brain would say to her, "Wow. This is so cool. How many scientists have the opportunity to study their own brains from the inside out?"

When her left brain faded into silence, she felt enormous and expansive. It was as if the limits of her body no longer contained her, and she felt a part of everything around her. It was as if she was pure energy. It was beautiful to her, and she was completely at peace. In her words, she said, "I felt like a genie liberated from its bottle. The energy of my spirit seemed to flow like a great whale gliding through a sea of silent euphoria."[ss]

She finally succeeded in contacting someone before she lost consciousness and was taken to the hospital. When she awoke several hours later, she felt as if she was suspended between two opposite planes of reality. All sensory input from light to sound caused intense pain. It seemed to her she would never be able to squeeze the enormity of herself into that tiny little body again. Somehow, though, she found the will to do so. She said to herself, "I'm still alive, and I have found Nirvana. And if I have found Nirvana and I'm still alive, then everyone who is alive can find Nirvana." She pictured a world filled with beautiful, compassionate, loving people who knew they could come to this space at any time. She realized what a tremendous gift she had been given, and the desire to share it with others motivated her to recover.

Brain surgery and eight years of therapy followed before she fully recovered. Today she says she is a new person—one who can step into the consciousness of her right hemisphere on command and be one with all that is. She now has a deep personal understanding based on an intimate experience of something she studied abstractly as a neuroscientist for years. That being the existence of two completely different personalities within everyone, with each personality situated within one of the two hemispheres of the brain. For most people the left brain (the calculating, logical, ego-driven part) is dominant. Therefore, the consciousness that arises from the right brain (the part that generates creativity, empathy, and connection) gets neglected. Taylor contends it is possible for human beings to create better lives for themselves and others by learning to bypass the left brain and actively engage with the capacities of the right brain.[TT]

She found an audience for this message. Her TED Talk entitled "My Stroke of Insight" has had over fourteen million viewings to date. Taylor described her experience of the stroke, when her left brain shut down, as nirvana. I bestowed the label "mystical experience."

That phrase seems to fit what she described because it meets the three criteria for a mystical experience William James laid out in his 1902 book *The Varieties of Religious Experience*—still considered the definitive text on the subject. First, according to James, a mystical experience is ineffable. It is so profound to the person who experiences it that it simply can't be described with words. It's like trying to describe how strawberries taste. It can't be fully imparted to another person. It can only be approximated. Second, James says the mystical experience has a noetic quality. This means the experience is deemed so profound to the person who experiences it that it eclipses all other sources of truth or knowledge. Third, it is a revelation. The experience itself carries a definite albeit curious sense of authority.[UU] Huston Smith added another generally accepted fourth quality to James's criteria. A mystical experience, though transient, stays with the person as a living memory and exhibits the power to change the person's life.[vv]

The common thread that runs through the mystical experiences of all traditions is oneness, connectedness, and unity that exists beyond the phenomenal universe. Mystics speak of this unity in many ways, and they often use the idioms and language of their own particular religious traditions. Therefore, they might or might not make reference to a deity. However, regardless of the culturally specific references in the language, the mystic's message always suggests there is a wholeness behind the way people ordinarily perceive themselves as discrete entities separate from the rest of creation. This experience of unity and connectedness usually carries with it great feelings of expansiveness, peacefulness, and bliss.

Many in the ranks of progressive religion cast skeptical eyes toward anything labeled mystical. This is not surprising since that the word "mystic" is etymologically related to "mystery." Many have come to depend on the rational, analytical parts of their brains to shape their world views in true Individuating Faith fashion. This tendency can become even more pronounced when they assess something as subjective and intangible as religion and spirituality. It should, therefore, be expected that many in a group where critical, independent thinking is prevalent might have some difficulties with spiritual or religious concepts shrouded in the mystical.

This suspicion of mysticism is actually one thing that some religious progressives (those at the Individuating Faith stage) have in common with fundamentalists. Both intellectually geared, scientifically minded individuals and rigid, dogmatic types who are only able to process in either-or categories tend to have the most difficulty with mystical thinking and ways of expression.

There are good reasons for being a bit circumspect when it comes to this business of mysticism. Not everything that makes people feel good and expansive and brings about some sentimental cosmic consciousness can be considered an authentic mystical experience. A good stiff drink or a few puffs of weed will usually bring about the same result. That's what I've been told anyway. I have no personal experience.

There are also plenty of amateur mystics out there spouting all sorts of new age gobbledygook. The Internet is saturated with them. Certainly they are often well meaning, but mysticism is much like art. Not everyone who takes brush in hand and splatters colors on a canvas is necessarily an artist. The true artist is one who has the heart and desire to devote years to such things as the study of composition and the mastery of technique. That person must then gain a great deal of experience working with a certain medium such as watercolors, acrylics, or oils. All this is just groundwork the serious artist must do to prepare for a vision or inspiration that might lead to the creation of a great work of art. The true mystic is also someone who has devoted years of serious time and energy to intense study of religious tradition. The mystic has learned to communicate using the language and idioms of that tradition and devoted much time to meditation or contemplative prayer. Just as discipline is required before any meaningful breakthrough in any craft or field of endeavor, so it is for that rare mystic whose vision is to be taken seriously. Just as great art has a certain formal definition in its compositions, so it is with profound mystical visions that garner the world's attention. Mystical visions come from within established traditions and speak to that tradition with an authority that can only be gained through mastery of both the tradition and the self.

Mysticism is largely experiential. Therefore, it draws its authority through grounding in experience. There's always been conflict between reason and experience as sources of religious authority even though both are included in the Wesleyan Quadrilateral (see chapter 6.) How does one reconcile reason with the experience of the mystic? How is that done when the experience comes second-hand? Not everyone can claim to have had a mystical experience. Yet all human beings have been given rational natures, and it would seem logical and consistent people would be expected to use them. In the aftermath of the Enlightenment, people began to increasingly engage with the powers of reason. It became the primary instrument in liberating humankind from the accumulated superstitions of religious traditions. Since the Enlightenment there has been a tendency (with ample justification) to move away from supernaturalism and toward science.

However, the mystical doesn't have to have any basis in the supernatural. We're not talking about walking on water or raising the dead. A mystic is simply someone who has an inner experience—someone who has gone off into the transcendent through the psyche and returned to tell about it. The transcendentalists Emerson, Thoreau, and Margaret Fuller all rejected the supernatural and any theology of miracles. However, all described the mystical in their writings and saw value in such experiences. To them mysticism meant an extraordinary state of consciousness where a person subjectively experiences oneness with that which transcends him or her. Emerson and Thoreau even left record of having such personal experiences while in nature.

However, just because the mystical experience is something subjective that can't be studied in rational ways, it doesn't mean people can't use intuition and plain common sense to separate the wheat from the chaff. As I go through my discernment process, I critically examine the message but also the life of the messenger. I ask myself several questions. Where does the mystic's vision lead? Is the message an honest search for truth, or is it meant to advance some special agenda? Is there an internal consistency to it? Does it bring about fuller integrity? Is it expansive and growth inducing or does it confine us to the limits of the familiar? Does it lead to greater connectedness between individuals and between the individual and the surrounding world? Is the vision an inclusive one? Has the mystical experience led the mystic into greater engagement with the world or to an escape from the world? Essential to our discernment is whether or not the mystic's vision makes the world a better, more compassionate, and more loving place.

Karen Armstrong, the author of several popular books in the religious field, has moved to a more mystical perspective in her personal faith. When she became acquainted with Jill Bolte Taylor's story, she noted the similarity of her story and the Buddha's. Like Taylor, Buddha was reluctant to return to this world. Like her, "he wanted to luxuriate in the sense of enlightenment." But, as Karen Armstrong continues, "The dynamic of the religious required that he go out into the world and share his sense of compassion."ʷʷ That same compassion is also why Taylor said she wrote her memoir.

Taylor brings a unique perspective to the world's ongoing conversation about mysticism. By virtue of her direct experience, she can speak to the subject from the inside while also speaking as a scientist. The juxtaposition of those two perspectives gives a commanding authority to her message that is surely needed in these jaded times.

To sum it all up, I can do no better than quote Taylor's closing remarks from her TED Talk.

"So who are we? We are the life force power of the universe, with manual dexterity and two cognitive minds. And we have the power to choose, moment by moment, who and how we want to be in the world. Right here, right now, I can step into the consciousness of my right hemisphere, where we are. I am the life force power of the universe. I am the life force power of the fifty trillion beautiful molecular geniuses that make up my form, at one with all that is. Or, I can choose to step into the consciousness of my left hemisphere, where I become a single individual, a solid. Separate from the flow, separate from you. I am Dr. Jill Bolte Taylor: intellectual, neuroanatomist. These are the 'we' inside of me. Which would you choose? Which do you choose? And when? I believe that the more time we spend choosing to run the deep inner peace circuitry of our right hemispheres, the more peace we will project into the world, and the more peaceful our planet will be."[xx]

Having a profound experience of both these parts of her consciousness and then coming away with the ability to choose at will the path to deep inner peace, Dr. Taylor is rather uniquely positioned to give the rest of us hope that we can choose that path as well. These two cognitive minds are present within everyone, whether a scientist, a mystic, or just an ordinary person who has a heart for a hurting world. We are the life force power of the universe. May everyone hearken to this message and put it into practice.

* * *

Part III

Growth and Compassion

fourteen

A Seminal Experience

Remember the experiment from grammar school where students took seeds of some sort and placed them in a glass with a paper towel? The students then put the glasses with the seeds on a sunny windowsill and added a little water to the bottom of the glass. The paper towel acted like a wick to keep the seeds moist, and over a couple weeks, the budding young scientists got to observe some of the seeds burst into halves. Tiny young sprouts emerged and started growing toward the rim of the glass.

There are many variations on this basic experiment where other seeds are deprived of light, heat, nutrients, or oxygen to observe the effect on germination. It was usually pretty obvious what would happen to the seeds deprived of one or more of these essential factors, and most students could write reports on the experiment without even bothering to measure the growth of the little sprouts. Nevertheless, this type of experiment served a useful function as one of the first introductions to the scientific method. It demonstrated the necessity of developing the powers of observation.

What really fascinated me about the experiment was watching how the germinated seeds would always burst open and split into two halves. Then this tiny plant would emerge from the seed and quickly grow much larger than the seed itself with nothing but water, light, and the scant nutrients stored in the seed. When seeds are planted in soil, all these processes are hidden. Doing the experiment seemed to me an engaging way to gain a window into one of the marvels of Mother Nature.

As I began to reflect on my seminary experience, my mind wandered back to some of the things I observed happening to those tiny seeds. The word "seminary" means a school that trains people to be ministers, priests, or rabbis. However, the word also means a seedbed. Nurseries sprout the seeds of young plants in a particular area designated as the seminary. "Seminary" and "seminal" (as in the seminal vesicle of the male reproductive tract or a seminal idea—a primary idea with numerous developmental possibilities) share the same Latin root.

Now that my time at Candler School of Theology is well behind me and time has furnished some perspective on my experiences there, I must admit the analogy of the seminary experience to young developing seeds is quite apt. For a great portion of my time at seminary, I was buried alive underneath a pile of books and papers. I found myself embedded in an environment where a steady stream of new words and ideas nurtured my development. Words such as hermeneutic, eschatology, exegetical, redaction, and epistemological became elements of everyday exchanges in this stimulating cultural milieu. I was never quite sure if I was using those words correctly. It just seemed as if it was expected I throw one or two into every paper. At least they made each paper sound important and scholarly, even if I had no idea what I was talking about.

One of the things I took away from my seminary experience was a new conviction regarding the power and influence of ideas. As I observed my classmates gain all this exposure to new and different ideas, I repeatedly noticed a curious phenomenon. Many students came to Candler with rather rigid notions about religion. (God said it. I believe it. That settles it. Or something of that sort.) Some were so convinced of the rightness of their beliefs they would launch into some rather spirited debates with the professors—until it became clear the professors totally outclassed them. After just a couple weeks, I came to expect certain questions to automatically come from certain parts of the room. After a few months, however, I noticed some changes in the arguments of some of these more outspoken classmates. The substance of their debates took on many of the new ideas they were exposed to. They had adopted ideas I remember them adamantly opposing – ideas which they now used to defend their new positions.

The influence of new ideas on the minds and spirits of some students seemed to work much like the light and warmth of the sun on those little seeds in the windowsill of my second-grade classroom. Those little seeds had stored potential for transformation. All it took was coming under the slow, steady influence of the sun's rays to work a small miracle. Day by day, that potentiality was released, and the class could actually see the growth of the young plants as the sun shone on them. The liberating effects of critical biblical scholarship seemed to work that way on the minds of some of my colleagues, much like the daylight working on those seeds to create transformations. Gaining exposure to more enlightened viewpoints gradually caused their minds to open just like the leaves on those little sprouts.

I will never forget a moment in my Old Testament survey class when the professor presented evidence that much of the Torah (the first five books of the Bible) actually came from four independent sources—the so-called JEDP sources. Modern biblical scholarship convincingly demonstrates that material from these four sources was arranged in parallel fashion and edited together to create a seamless document. This is evident in the two creation stories at the beginning of Genesis. One is from Genesis 1:1 to 2:4, and the second begins with Genesis 2:5. They are two independent stories from two of these JEDP sources. Both use different vocabulary and names for God and humanity and have entirely different viewpoints and agendas. This is even more prominent in the two stories of God's covenant with Abraham. One is in Genesis 15, and another is in Genesis 17.[YY]

The class was about four weeks into the first semester when the professor presented this evidence. In a classroom of 160 students, I could have heard a pin drop. I could sense the foundations of many people's faith crumbling around me. It seemed to disturb many that much of the Torah is a collection of Babylonian and Akkadian myths that were appropriated and then creatively and artistically edited together to create the present document. Evidence that similar elementary ideas informed many early civilizations only served to strengthen my faith in the power of these stories. Yet it seemed to profoundly disturb those whose faith rested on the conviction that the Bible was directly dictated verbatim from God's mouth.

Reflecting on this experience caused me to think again about those little beans on the windowsill. No matter how the seeds were positioned, when the sprout emerged, it would automatically turn and grow up, and the roots would turn and grow down. No matter where seeds germinate, gravity has the universal ability to orient the young plants in the world. These mythic stories in the Bible function upon the human psyche just like gravity on seeds. The stories have gravitas, and this accounts for their longevity and perseverance as parts of human culture.

I learned some interesting things in seminary. I might not have taken away all of the finer points of theology, but I learned that the human spirit is amenable to the influence of a more enlightened approach to religion. I learned something of the influence of ideas when they are properly framed and articulated with reason and conviction. The more we understand the mythic and imaginative basis of all faiths, the more likely we are to recognize the possibility that the faiths of other peoples might have common ground with ours. Coming to better understand these commonalities makes us a better conversation partner in dialogue with others when religious differences surface. Better understanding of the faith and values of others also facilitates the process whereby we become a more compassionate person. Compassion is to "feel with" another. (Com means "with," passion means "feel")

This seminary experience teaches the importance of continuing dialogue, even when initially there seems to be no perceptible change in others when we share ideas. The human mind and spirit are seedbeds of potential growth toward a future with more peace and justice. Though we might not think there is any effect on others when we share the basis of our faith, many things might be going on with others under the surface, things that are not immediately accessible and observable by us. If what we do and say to others nourishes the human spirit in healthy ways and our way of living our faith sheds compassionate light on the human situation, who knows? Light can facilitate growth. New ideas can expand the intellectual and emotional space where it feels safe and freer choices can be made. There can be more room for truth – about ourselves and about our worlds. There can be growth.

* * *

fifteen

Can We Talk?

Let's say you are going to throw a big party, so you invite a lot of people. Some of them you know really well, and some you do not really know at all. On the night of the party, one of these people you hardly know comes into town. When the person arrives, he or she is unable to find your house. The person stops at a phone booth at the edge of town and calls you. What are you going to do? If you said, "I'm going to tell that person where I live," you would be wrong. That is not what you would do—at least not at first. If you tell that person where you live, it will make no sense. The person is from somewhere else, so he or she likely has no frame of reference from which to navigate. What you are going to do is find out where that person is. Having established that, you can carefully proceed to tell him or her how to get from their present location to where you are.

When I'm in this situation, it's usually important to me that my guests arrive as soon as possible in relatively good spirits. Therefore, I expend no small amount of mental energy in making sure my directions are as clear, concise, and simple as possible. Since that's what I put most of my effort into, that's the thing I remember most—not the first part about finding out where that person is. However, that's the really crucial piece. Without beginning my thought process there, it doesn't matter how much I know about my town. I might know it backward and forward, but that's of no use to the person unless I first locate him or her.

While true for giving directions, it's even more important to begin conversations about religious faith in much the same way. One must begin by finding out where the other person is. When one begins by sharing where he or she is, there might not be a common frame of reference for the other to navigate by. How can that person possibly understand how to get from his or her location to the other? In the case of spiritual geography, though, many don't automatically function as they would with their lost guests. It's not one's tendency to first locate others in relation to where he or she is spiritually.

So how can we proceed? How can we find out where others are and let them know where we are as we attempt to have conversations? The type of listening necessary for meaningful conversation requires a quiet mind—something like living out a meditation. A quiet mind is relatively free of the automatic responses that characterize many people who think critically. Religious progressives often pride themselves in the ability to think freely and critically. I don't necessarily disparage that. That critical thinking has continually put us at the forefront of social issues throughout recent history—labor and education reform, civil rights, and marriage rights. However, recognize that critical thinking is a double-edged sword. That same critical thinking is responsible for a lot of our mental background noise when confronted with someone at a very different place. Often in conversation with someone who is in a different place spiritually I stop listening. In my attempts at conversation, those internal voices keep telling me to tell the other person where I am rather than stopping and listening to find out where he or she is. I know the other person's internal voices are speaking loudly also. As in the story of the acquaintance who wants to come to your party, it seems as if that guest is standing in a phone booth located on a crowded street corner. It is hard to hear because of all that background noise of convictions, experiences, and prejudices. However, ask yourself if you are free enough in your thinking to hear past your own background noise to find out if the person really wants to come to the party. Are you free enough of that noise to start a conversation?

Perhaps the answer is right there in the word "conversation" itself. Take apart the word converse. "Con" means "with," and "verse" means "song." When people converse, therefore, as opposed to merely talking, the word itself suggests the encounter be reminiscent of the harmonies and rhythms of a musical composition.

I will never forget a special moment from my seminary years. To understand this moment, you must realize that when I felt compelled to go off to study theology, my decision was partly based on the romantic idea that seminary would include a lot of informal conversations with classmates about life and meaning and late afternoons at one of the taverns in Emory Village sipping a beer with some of the professors and talking about Jesus. One of my mentors planted this notion, but he had attended seminary twenty-five years before. His seminary years were an age when the life of a seminary professor allowed time for such fraternal relationships. At any rate, not many such collegial encounters with the professors punctuated my seminary experience. There were some moments, though – such as this one.

One of my church history professors took the students out for coffee one morning after class, and the professor and I ended up enjoying our second cup together alone, as everyone else had to leave for another class. I asked him some questions about his background and how he came to be a seminary professor. He already knew I was preparing for a second career as a minister. After he gave me a brief summary of his professional journey, which eventually led to him teaching theology, he confided that he envied me very much because I was able to really say what was on my mind. Apparently he had actually been taking note during those few times I ventured to speak out in class. Then he said, "I'm not sure I really believe the theological perspective from which I teach. Sometimes I feel as if I am merely talking to myself when I'm up there in front of the class. It's like I'm trying to convince myself to buy into the party line of the church that pays my salary and funds my retirement." Then he proceeded to ask me a few questions about my faith journey and what convinced me to pursue a career in ministry midlife. We had a conversation. The measures of our lives came together in a blending of voices that resulted in a joyful experience for both. There was a similarity that came out of the depths of our human experience that allowed us to find a certain harmony. Our time together was, metaphorically, "with song."

The word "converse" can also be dissected in another way. Notice how similar it is to "convert." Their Latin roots are the same. *Convertari* is to turn around or to change. This implies that to converse with someone is to invite the possibility that you might convert that person or, God help us, actually be converted yourself. Some people (myself included) have trouble with this idea of conversion. Perhaps it is because many have fled from religious experiences and environments where they were subjected to the attempts of individuals and groups to convert them to their ways of thinking or to a particular creed or dogma. As a recipient of that particular type of religious abuse, I am very likely to resent and avoid any kind of dialogue where someone is trying to "fix" me by trying to convert me to a particular belief or doctrine. To have a true conversation, though, we must be willing to extend ourselves and hear others. Sometimes this involves hearing beyond the particular words they use. For a conversation to occur, a safe space must be created so the other person feels comfortable and secure enough to reveal themselves and share what is on his or her heart. Often this requires that we bracket certain convictions and certainties when these are very different or even opposed to those of our conversation partner. This is not easy, especially when it concerns things we feel passionate about.

When I was a chaplain at Emory Hospital doing my clinical pastoral education, I was confronted with a patient. I'll call him Chuck. Chuck held convictions very different than mine. He was on my floor, though, and I was to be his minister. When I first met Chuck, he asked me what church I belonged to. I told him I was a Unitarian. He immediately went on a diatribe about...shall we say... people of a different sexual orientation than him. It was very difficult to be in the room in the midst of such prejudice. The tragic thing about Chuck, besides having a heart filled with such fear and hate, was that he was dying from an advanced form of kidney cancer.

As I reviewed my patients with my supervisor later that day, I told her about my encounter with Chuck. I told her I did not think I was the best person to minister to him. She proceeded to tell me in her very Zen way the story that opens this chapter about throwing a party. She encouraged me to stay with Chuck. She told me I could learn a lot about how to listen from him. So I did.

The next day I made my rounds, and I listened. I listened beyond Chuck's hatred to what he was really afraid of. I learned he was afraid of dying, and he was afraid of dying alone. So many people in his life had abandoned him. All his bitterness gave way to sadness and tears. He became a human being right before my eyes— one I could feel genuine empathy for.

To stand in the presence of someone with a different theology and ideology is sometimes very difficult. Sometimes it is uncomfortable to turn to meet another human being when people hold so tightly to their principles. I'm not talking about turning one's back on hard-won convictions; I'm just talking about turning to hear the other person.

It would have been so much easier if I could have converted Chuck to my way of thinking. It would have relieved me of my discomfort, and I could have cast myself as his savior. There was no time for that, though. Chuck died a couple days later. I have no idea where he was with his hatred and bitterness when he died, but I do know his heart softened enough for me to find a human being beneath it all, and all I did was listen. I found out where he was. By quieting my inner voices that kept telling me to tell him where I was, I just listened. I listened for the voice deep within Chuck that wanted to come to the party but did not know where it was.

What if everyone could wear beliefs and convictions like casual dress rather than a suit of armor? It would be so much easier to move about in the thoughts of another and discover commonalities. What if we began every conversation with a sincere effort to bracket our own convictions and make a sincere effort to find out where the other person is? If we could learn to do these things, what freedom we would have. The places that would feel safe and joyful in relationships would expand exponentially. When both parties in a conversation learn and experience this, healing and conversion can happen because no one is intentionally *trying* to fix or convert the other.

In my quest for conversation and community, I have been a part of several groups where I have been transformed, and I have been given the grace to be a transforming presence for others. That is what ministry is all about. That is what love is about. Because of the yearning of the human heart for peace and understanding, within everyone is a capacity for transformation, for turning, and for conversion. It can be evoked. There are certain conditions that must be met, though, such as time for silence and a certain amount of mutual trust and respect. If our values include regarding every person as having inherent worth and dignity, then turning toward others is never a turning away from personal convictions.

There is goodness in every human heart. People just need to learn how to listen for it. It does not always come easily or naturally. Sometimes it takes a lot of scratching below the surface, but the conversation is always interesting and challenging. Are you ready for this type of challenge in your dialogue with others? This type of radical listening might be just what is needed to revive some of those encounters that seem dull. It might even be a way to change that sinking feeling when a certain person walks in the room—the one who induces eye rolling and casting about for a back door. Next time see if you can listen that person into being more genuine. Quiet the voices in your mind that orient you to the world, and start getting a little more information about where that person is. Who knows? If you persist, that person might want to join your party and have a conversation.

* * *

sixteen

Discerning the Call

"When they had finished breakfast, Jesus said to Simon Peter, 'Simon son of John, do you love me more than these?' He said to him, 'Yes, Lord; you know that I love you.' Jesus said to him, 'Feed my lambs.' A second time he said to him, 'Simon son of John, do you love me?' He said to him, 'Yes, Lord; you know that I love you.' Jesus said to him, 'Tend my sheep.' He said to him the third time, 'Simon son of John, do you love me?' Peter felt hurt because he said to him the third time, 'Do you love me?' And he said to him, 'Lord, you know everything; you know that I love you.' Jesus said to him, 'Feed my sheep.'"
—John 21:15–17 (New Revised Standard Version)

I would like to tell a story by the Russian novelist Leo Tolstoy. No, it's not *War and Peace*. It's not nearly that long, so bear with me. It's called "Two Old Men." In the story two old men are friends, and they decide to fulfill a promise they made together many years before to go on a pilgrimage to worship God in Jerusalem. On the way they cross a land in the midst of a famine, and they meet a family near starvation. The first old man can't be deterred from his journey. After all, he's going to worship God. He continues on his way to Jerusalem the next morning. The second old man stays reluctantly behind to do what he can for this family. What starts out as a simple gesture of offering bread and water gradually turns into a long-term commitment as his love for them deepens, and one problem turns into another. He helps them get back on their feet, buys seed for them to plant crops, and cooks for them until they are able to do it for themselves. He says to himself, "Unless I stay this family will end up back as I found them. And if I leave to go seek God beyond the sea, I might lose God in myself." He ends up staying with this family for months until they regain their strength, and then he makes sure they have the provisions they need to make it through the next winter. As he spends time with this family, they become quite attached to him, and he comes to care deeply for them as well. Finally the day comes when he is able to continue on his journey, but by this time his money is almost gone. He is unable to continue to Jerusalem and has to return home.

Once home the two old men meet up again. The first old man is back from the Holy Land, and he swears he has seen the second old man in Jerusalem at several of the holy shrines. Each time he saw his friend, the crowds of pilgrims prevented him from getting close enough to speak, but he could tell it was his friend. On each of these occasions, he saw an aura about his friend as if he were an angel. The second old man, whose money and energy were spent in service to the poor family and who never made it to Jerusalem, just changes the subject.[zz]

One could say the first old man visited the Holy Land as a tourist. The second man went on a pilgrimage and became holy. The first sought the sacred in expected ways and expected places. The second was open to the divine as it presented itself to him, and thereby his acts of service turned the place where he found himself into holy ground.

Serving can be understood as a vocation. The word "vocation" comes from the Latin *vocare*—to call. I mean, therefore, the thing God calls each person to do. There are a lot of different voices calling in every life. Our bodies call to us through biology. I must provide my daily bread. I must make a living for myself and my family. There is the call of reason. If I do what seems right in this situation, I might lose my job. There is also the voice of responsibility. This is often heard as the voice of "ought." I ought to go to church. I ought to go into Christian service. A big one is the call of guilt. Perhaps I can make up for some of my wrongs by doing this thing or that for God. There is even the call of the ego. I'm sure everyone has come across someone on TV or reality who seems to have been called into the ministry more by ego than by God. Perhaps this sounds harsh and judgmental, but in all honesty, it does occur to me when I see some of the gross distortions of energy and resources that go into some of the ministries of certain celebrity ministers.

Discerning the call of God from the calls of these other things is not always easy. Ministering to others in any capacity is a holy call. It is a call from God who only calls people to holiness, wholeness, and healthiness. (All these words share the same root as "holy.") The motivation to minister comes from that innermost part of being that some refer to as a "soul." Finding one's true call is one of the most joyous things that can happen to a human being. That doesn't mean it will always be a source of happiness. Sometimes unhappiness will come with it. However, there is something called joy that goes beyond happiness, and it becomes a slow burning rapture within. This is the satisfaction of doing what God intended, and that transcends mere superficial pleasure.

The theologian Frederick Buechner says vocation is where deep gladness meets the world's deep need. In other words, for work to be a vocation it must meet two requirements. It must bring the person the most joy, and the world must need the person to do it. When these things align, work is a vocation. Many have done work at some time that meets a need in the world. Maybe it was flipping burgers, driving a truck, teaching, or running a business. However, if that job was tedious and boring, it did not meet the first requirement—being joyous. On the other hand, if someone is doing a job such as writing jingles for beer commercials, then it might be work that person really enjoys. However, it probably does not meet requirement two—filling a deep need in the world.

In Tolstoy's story the second old man who stayed with the family and served them is someone who likely found his vocation. Obviously he was meeting deep needs from the very beginning in rescuing these poor people from starvation. As he did the work, though, he began to find a deep joy in serving, and this joy made the work into a joyous vocation. His friend, the first old man, began to see the second old man in the holy places when the second old man discovered the sacred dimension in the everyday tasks he was performing for the family. By both meeting a need and finding gladness, the second old man found a divine call. This is when the first old man began to see the aura about the second old man as he caught those mysterious glimpses of him in Jerusalem.

The curious conversation between Jesus and Peter quoted at the beginning of this chapter has been interpreted in many ways. Many scriptural authorities make much of Jesus telling Peter three times to feed his sheep. It is as if Jesus is intentionally berating Peter by referencing that he had denied Jesus three times. I think there is a deeper significance to the conversation, though. Peter was a sort of leader of the disciples. He was in the inner circle of those disciples who were there for events of particular significance. For instance, Peter was there along with James and John for the trans-figuration when Jesus went up on the mountain and appeared in his glory with Moses and Elijah—an event mentioned in all three of the synoptic gospels. Peter wanted to stay there in that holy place, and he asked Jesus if they could make three tents—for Jesus and the two prophets. In another instance at the Last Supper, Peter initially refused to have Jesus wash his feet. When Jesus told him that unless he allowed him to wash his feet, then Peter could have no part in him, Peter wanted Jesus to wash his feet, hands, and head. Peter always seemed to relish being in the special moments and in the special, holy places. Peter is much like the first old man in the story who wanted to go to Jerusalem to be in the holy place.

It is an admirable thing to set off on a pilgrimage to Jerusalem or to want to be in a holy place or office, and I do not mean to disparage such an effort or intention. Jesus, however, wanted Peter to recognize there is more. There is a higher calling, and it can count for joy. Peter, if you love me, feed my sheep. It is as if Jesus is saying that love for me is in the care and concern you show my flock. Feed my sheep. If love for me is your deep gladness, then in that love you will find yourself meeting the world's deep need—by feeding me when I am hungry, giving me drink when I am thirsty, welcoming me when I am a stranger, clothing me when I am naked, taking care of me when I am sick, and visiting me when I am in prison. Feed my sheep. In that service you will find yourself in a holy place. When you find the place within yourself and experience deep gladness in these acts, you will have found your true calling. From there you will shine forth just as the second old man in the story. Feed my sheep.

* * *

seventeen

The Lost Art of
Welcoming the Soul

The Bible describes Job as a "blameless, upright man who loved God and turned away from evil."[14] Job is also a very wealthy and prosperous man measured by the currency of his time. He possesses five hundred oxen, seven thousand sheep, and three thousand camels. He has ten children—seven sons and three daughters. Life has been very good to him.

One day, though. Job receives report after report of devastating news. First, he is told fire has killed his numerous livestock and thousands of camels. That's like the stock market going from sixteen thousand to zero overnight. Next he hears bandits have killed his many servants. That news just reaches him when he learns a tornado blew down the house where his sons and daughters were gathered and killed them all.

Upon hearing all this, Job is as faithful as he has always been. He falls to the ground and worships God. "Naked I came from my mother's womb, and naked shall I return there," he prays. "The

---

14 Job 1:1.

Lord gave and the Lord has taken away; blessed be the name of the Lord."[15]

Job's shell-shocked response to his life-changing tragedies seems to be a passive acceptance of his fate. However, those words were uttered in the first numbing shock of grief and do not sustain him for long.

Stripped of family and worldly possessions, Job becomes infected with what the Bible describes as "loathsome sores from the sole of his feet to the crown of his head."[16] This is too much. He is no longer able to quietly accept his fate. Job begins to curse the day he was born, and he cries out "Why me, Lord?" He demands to know why these things have happened.

Job's friends hear about these terrible tragedies. Like good friends should, they come to visit Job. The scripture reads, "Now when Job's three friends heard of all these troubles that had come upon him, each of them set out from his home—Eliphaz the Temanite, Bildad the Shuhite, and Zophar the Naamathite. They met together to go and console and comfort him. When they saw him from a distance, they did not recognize him, and they raised their voices and wept aloud; they tore their robes and threw dust in the air upon their heads. They sat with him on the ground seven days and seven nights, and no one spoke a word to him, for they saw that his suffering was very great"[17]

However, Job's friends, who initially sat with him in his grief, begin to get a bit nervous when Job starts questioning God and getting angry with him. The friends leap to God's defense and offer explanations for why God has let these tragedies occur. In doing so they offer good examples of how *not* to do pastoral care.

---

15 Job 1:21.
16 Job 2:7.
17 Job 2:11–13.

"You must have sinned greatly for this to happen," the first friend says. "You better repent." The second friend offers his own explanation. "Think of it as a growing experience. You'll be so much stronger because of it." The third friend is much more direct with Job. "How dare you question God?" he says. "This must be God's will, and who are you to question it?"[18]

Job does not accept any of his friends' explanations or attempts to console him. Job lashes out at his friends by saying, "But I would speak to the Almighty, and I desire to argue my case with God. As for you, you whitewash with lies; all of you are worthless physicians. If you would only keep silent, that would be your wisdom!"[19] In other words Job tells his friends they are cold comfort to him, and they can just buzz off.

Have you ever experienced the type of care and comfort Job's friends tried to offer him? Perhaps it was after the loss of a loved one. Someone comes up to you and says, "He or she is in a better place now" or, "He or she has gone to be with Jesus." Perhaps you were going through some other crisis such as the loss of a job, a divorce, or some other relationship crisis. Someone comes up to you with the best of intentions and says something like, "I know how you feel" or, "That happened to me once, and I found I just needed to pray about it." Perhaps this person says, "Maybe God is trying to teach you something." That one really makes you feel good. Doesn't it?

Instead of making one feel better, so many of the things said during a difficult time end up making us feel worse. It's a common problem, and it doesn't just come from well-meaning but misguided members of the Christian community. Secular society is also guilty.

So how can one respond to a friend going through a difficult time? How can one show more love and compassion as part of a

---

18   Brief paraphrase of Job 4-11.
19   Job 13:3-5.

caring community? These are questions everyone should wrestle with. Even ministers trained in the art of pastoral care and aware of the dangers and pitfalls struggle with these questions.

Perhaps there is a lesson to learn from Job's comforters. Let's look again at the story. Even though Job's three friends end up looking pretty bad, they started off rather well. They showed up, and that alone is not always easy when someone dear is hurting. Many cultures, including the Judeo-Christian one, tends to deny disease, death, and suffering. It becomes easy to say, "That person would probably rather be left alone right now." There might be some truth to that, and one should always be sensitive to a person's need for solitude. However, at some point friends will want to hear from their friends. It's called a ministry of presence. Just being present for a friend can be a great gift.

Job's friends also grieved along with Job. The text says they wept aloud, tore their robes, and threw dust upon their heads. All these actions were signs of mourning in the ancient world. His friends were willing to share in Job's grief and sorrow.

They were even willing to sit with Job in silence. The text says "no one spoke a word to him, for they saw that his suffering was very great."[20] Showing a person we care doesn't necessarily require words. Just sitting with someone who is ill or grieving can be a powerful act. It's only when his friends spoke that things went wrong. Sometimes any words beyond "I'm sorry" detract from the intent to be comforting and consoling.

It can sometimes be difficult to discern when silence is the appropriate response. Often there is pressure to say something, even though better instincts say words are superfluous. This pressure to say something—anything—when there is nothing to say sometimes compels people to stay away when friends are hurting. I've experienced that also, even as a minister.

---

20 Job 2:13.

There is a fourth thing Job's friends did right. They gave Job the time and space to speak first. The text tells us they gave him a week. They sat in silence with him for that long before anyone spoke. When Job did speak, he began to curse the day of his birth and to cry out to God in anger. His friends formulated their responses rather than simply sitting with his words and listening to the meaning and emotion behind them. One of the most common impediments to good listening happens because we only listen to the other person long enough to hear something that triggers a response. Then we turn our attention to what we have to say and begin to look for a pause or an opening to get it into the conversation.

Why are people compelled to say or do something for friends at times such as these? It's not too difficult to understand. My friend is hurting. I care a lot about my friend, and since my friend is hurting, that makes me hurt too. If I can fix the pain or the situation quickly, then I won't have to hurt anymore. So it seems much easier to offer some sort of quick answer or platitude rather than doing the most compassionate but also most difficult thing—simply sitting there and sharing the pain.

When Job's friends spoke, it was out of love and concern. However, they spoke from their own ideologies and theologies rather than simply making room in their hearts and minds to listen to Job. His friends' well-intentioned responses were still efforts to convert Job to their ways of thinking. The answers they had worked out for why bad things happen to good people didn't work for Job, though. The answers I might offer someone at a time such as that are no more likely to be of any comfort than Job's friends' advice. It is human nature to want to offer hard-won ideology or theology during difficult times because people sense pain and vulnerability in their friends. It is much easier to offer my answers to life's difficult questions than to make room in my heart and mind as my friend works out a way forward. After all, if my friend's understanding or belief turns out to be different from mine, it is likely to call mine into question. Therefore, many efforts to fix, heal, or convert others are ultimately self-centered and unlikely to be of any real benefit to anyone.

The message here has a much broader application than just offering solace to a grieving friend. It offers a loving, compassionate way to be in community with others. Once people make room for others in their hearts and minds, they can sit with grieving friends or even someone who is angry, lonely, or simply searching for a place to call home. It is a way to create a welcoming, loving, and compassionate place for others.

We live in the age of electronic communications and social media such as Facebook and people have the opportunity to be more connected to each other than ever. Yet one of the most common laments is that no one seems to hear or understand us. How ironic. Parker Palmer is a Quaker teacher and author who endeavors to convey to the contemporary world the dynamics of Quaker spirituality and their sensitivity to the "still, small voice" of each person's inner light. Palmer says the fundamental problem is that the current ways of listening and speaking are instrumental rather than expressive. That is, people listen with intellect and ego, and people speak to the intellect and ego of the conversation partner. People don't endeavor to make every conversation a meeting of souls. If this doesn't resonate, take note the next time you are in conversation with someone else. Be mindful of how much of the dialogue consists of informing, affirming, rebuking, or trying to find common ground. These are hallmarks of conversing instrumentally. People are trying to convince others about their own opinions, ideas, and beliefs. At the very least, they are attempting to reinforce or persuade the others that they are really good people. According to Palmer's approach, people need receptive listening to be more welcoming of others. In receptive listening people give others time and space to speak their truths without any compulsion to insert their perspectives into the conversation.[AAA] By responding to others without commentary but deep listening to the intent and emotions behind their words, sometimes people can "listen the soul into being." It is something that is almost never modeled in today's world and is fast becoming a lost art.

Poets are usually more adept at expressing things such as deep listening than others. The following one conveys the essence of what it means to listen in a way that welcomes the soul. If you've read it before, I invite you to reflect on it again as if for the first time.

"Listen"

When I ask you to listen to me
And you start giving me advice,
You have not done what I asked.
When I ask you to listen to me
And you begin to tell me "why" I shouldn't feel that way,
You are trampling on my feelings.
When I ask you to listen to me
And you feel you have to do something to
solve my problems,
You have failed me, strange as that may seem.
Listen! All I ask is that you listen;
Not talk, nor do—just hear me.
And I can do for myself—I'm not helpless
When you do something for me, that I can
and need to do for myself,
You contribute to my fear and weakness.
But when you accept as a simple fact that I do feel what
I feel,
No matter how irrational

Then I quit trying to convince you
And can get about the business of understanding
What's behind this irrational feeling.
When that's clear,
The answers are obvious and I don't need advice.
Irrational feelings make sense when we
Understand what's behind them.
Perhaps that's why prayer works sometimes for
some people;
because God is mute, and doesn't give
advice to try to "fix" things,
He/she just listens, and lets you work it out
for yourself.
So please listen, and just hear me, and if you
want to talk,
Wait a minute for your turn,
And I'll listen to you.
—*Anonymous*

(A mental health consumer who was institutionalized over a number of years in Queensland wrote this poem. He wishes to remain anonymous.)

What would our lives be like, what would our congregations be like, and what would the world around us be like if just a few of us could really learn to listen to each other in this way? It seems this is what Job cried out for when he felt forsaken by God and everybody. It seems to be what the world hungers for with the laments that no one seems to hear or understand us. What if we could learn to listen without attempting to fix and be open in ways that are welcoming to the soul?

* * *

eighteen

The Canary in the Coal Mine

There is a relatively rare medical oddity known as situs inversus where the organs in the body are located on the side opposite to where they are usually found. The heart is on the right side of the chest rather than the left. The liver and appendix are on the left side rather than the right, and so forth. It's as if the body is a mirror image of what is regarded as the norm. Though situated abnormally, these organs function normally, so someone might be unaware he or she has this condition until a physician closely examines him or her.

One day the father of several children brought one into the emergency room and demanded to know what was wrong with him. Attempting to calm the obviously exasperated father, the doctor slowly and carefully examined the child. Rather reluctantly the doctor confessed he really could not find anything wrong with the child. Being careful not to alarm the father, he calmly explained that the child's heartbeat was louder on the right side of the chest than on the left. He said this might indicate the child had an unusual condition known as situs inversus, but this would not cause the child any problems. He would be able to lead a normal life. The father then turned and shouted to his wife, who was waiting out in the hall with the other children, "OK, honey. I finally found a doctor who knows what he's doing. Now you can bring in the one who is *really* sick."

Discerning competence in those who would offer their ministrations is sometimes a difficult task. This father discovered a way to discern which physician was knowledgeable and deliberate enough in his evaluation to trust with the ill child. Most do not have the advantage this father had of having another child to use as a test case. It is sometimes hard to find trustworthy, competent care in the medical community. The story strikes a note of humor because it represents a test that many would like to administer to a physician before placing their trust in him or her—a sort of quality assurance exam from the patient's perspective. People might not have perfect test cases readily available as this father did, but people make choices and distinctions every day using the same basic principle.

A person observes how another is treated, and on this basis he or she forms some opinion of the caretaker based on the care, concern, and competence these observations demonstrate. If there is an overlooked, neglected, or even maligned population, and there is a community that takes them in, cares for them, and treats them in ways that demonstrate respect, does that not function as a test case? By observing how people treat other people, especially marginalized people, it is possible to discern the depth of those people's spirituality and growth.

Though sometimes hard to find people to trust with the body, it seems even more difficult to find a community to entrust the soul. There are individuals and groups in the medical field who are not particularly healthy to be around, but in the spiritual field, it is also easy to fall into the hands of noxious individuals and groups. Discernment along the spiritual path is admittedly difficult and, as I can testify from personal experience, fraught with pitfalls. Sometimes it seems we have nothing more than trial and error to depend on as we seek out guides and companions along life's journey.

Here are four guidelines I have found helpful as I have learned to discern the people and groups it is most edifying for me to be with.

First, I look at their motivations. Does love seem to motivate them? By love I do not mean I get warm, fuzzy feelings every time I am in their presence. Groups that offer handshakes, hugs, and pats on the back are a dime a dozen. By love I mean something more. I find Scott Peck's definition of love especially appropriate for this type of discernment. He said in *The Road Less Traveled*, love is "the will to extend one's self for the purpose of nurturing one's own or another's spiritual growth."[BBB] Two comments about this definition might clarify it somewhat. First, in this sense love is not a feeling— at least not primarily. Second, since it is an act of the will, it requires effort, courage, and even risk. Therefore, a group that does not consider its members valuable enough to extend or exert itself for in sometimes extraordinary ways does not meet this criteria. Of course, a group can be motivated to exert itself for its members for reasons besides the nurturing of spiritual growth, so careful attention to the spoken and unspoken intentions of a group's action is necessary. I have been a part of groups whose prime motivations seemed to be glorifying a particular charismatic leader or the perpetuation of their institutional structures. Group motivations are usually fairly easy to spot by watching the flow of energy and money within the group.

Second, I look at the outcome of being in the group. What kind of effect does the group seem to have on its members and how they engage with the world around them? Does their participation in the group seem to make them more caring, socially responsible individuals, or does it seem to make them interested in gathering in their tight enclave again and again for no purpose higher than the mere pleasure of being together? Generally spiritual discernment of individuals and groups can proceed by applying the maxim of "Judge me not by my beliefs but by what my beliefs make of me."

Third, I look at the ideology of the group. Do I find the statements I hear group members profess congruent with my own? Discerning the degree to which this characteristic needs to be present can be a bit tricky. After all, part of choosing a group that is psychologically and spiritually right means that the group will challenge its members in some way. Therefore, perfect agreement between beliefs is not necessarily desired. For the group to contribute to one's spiritual development the presence of someone farther along the path toward a more integrated, whole, and accepting human being is necessary.

Perfect harmony between one and the group is not necessarily to be desired for another reason. I have encountered some groups and individuals where I found their values and professed beliefs compatible to my own, yet there seemed to be something missing. What the group overtly professed as its intention did not match what it professed in action. On the other hand, I have also encountered some groups with what I would consider some rather strange ideas, but their behavior showed a great depth of concern for the poor and the environment. Sometimes the fruits these groups bear in the world have caused me to reexamine a faith stance. What groups manifest through their actions tells me much more than what their verbalized values and ideals ever could.

Fourth, I ask myself how spiritually healthy the dynamics among the group members seem to be. Do the members respect each other or take every occasion to talk about one other behind each other's back? Does one person dominate, or are all gifts and graces acknowledged and sought? Do they demand politeness at all cost, or do they gently confront each other when necessary? One does not have to participate in a group too long before these things become apparent, and these patterns tell a great deal about the group's health and how far advanced its members are spiritually.

These four principles crystallize in the teachings of some of the greatest spiritual guides. Buddha visits a monastery and sees a monk ill with dysentery whom no one is helping. When he asks why, he is told the monk did nothing for them, so they saw no reason to help him. Buddha replies, "If you do not tend one another, then who is there to tend you? Whoever would tend me, he should tend the sick."[21] In his teachings to his disciples, Jesus said, "I was a stranger and you welcomed me, I was naked and you gave me clothing, I was sick and you took care of me, I was in prison and you visited me." The disciples seemed not to understand the point of the teaching and asked, "When was it that we saw you [as] a stranger and welcomed you, or naked and gave you clothing? And when was it that we saw you sick or in prison and visited you?" Jesus said, "Just as you did it to one of the least of these [indicating the multitudes around them], you did it to me."[22]

Both these teachers saw themselves as connected to each and every other human being. This is the essence of their great moral wisdom. In the way people treat others and offer hospitality to them, even "the least of these," people are demonstrating a radical understanding of the unity that underlies all humanity. A spirituality that recognizes this oneness and acts out of this oneness is at the heart of all the great mystical teachings. To serve the other with the best of our talents and abilities is to recognize that which is holy and to be revered in everybody.

---

21 Vinaya, Mahavagga 8.26.3.
22 Matt. 25:35–40.

One of my seminary professors, an Old Testament professor named Walter Brueggemann, offered a prophetic voice that advocated the type of radical hospitality of Jesus and the Buddha. He taught a parable where members of the gay and lesbian community functioned as a sort of canary in the coal mine for society. Coal miners used to take a caged canary into the mines with them as an early indicator of toxic gases. In a similar way, members of the gay community and other oppressed people are most likely to suffer the toxic effects of bigotry and injustice. How groups treat society's marginalized gives fair warning of whether, by joining that group, one risks exposure to a noxious environment. In a way, therefore, we do have the advantage of that father with the child who had situs inversus. By noting how organizations and communities treat the marginalized, one gets clear indications of how spiritually healthy these groups are and whether it is healthy to be a part of them. I have found this rule of thumb invaluable in discerning the direction to take on my spiritual path.

As we search for a spiritual community, one that, in the words of the father in the story at the beginning of this chapter "knows what its doing," we must ask ourselves questions. Is this community creating, in the sentiments of my Old Testament professor, a place where all of life's canaries can sing joyfully? Does this group do their utmost to demonstrate care, concern, and competence in the way they treat others—especially those pushed to the fringes of society such as poor, minority, or gay groups? When we seek out religious communities, we should look for more than just places to come together to recite great words. We should also notice actions. Judge the community not by its beliefs; judge it by what its beliefs make of it. Take account of how groups treat us and others—especially "the least of these." By observing, we can gain great insight into the group's principles as well as gain a fairly good assessment of where it stands on some pretty hefty

issues such as justice, mercy, and sacrificial love. The real lit-
mus test of faith comes down to how that faith engages with the
world and meets the world's great needs for love, acceptance and
hospitality.

* * *

Part IV

God

nineteen

God in the Third Dimension

There is a charming story called "Flatland" told by a nineteenth-century mathematician named Edwin Abott. Flatland is a two-dimensional world, and all the flat geometric shapes inhabit it—squares, triangles, circles, and so forth. One day the square who lives in this two-dimensional world is visited by a sphere from a three-dimensional world called Spaceland. However, all the square can see of the sphere is a circle—the part of the sphere that exists in his plane of existence. The square is amazed that its new acquaintance is able to grow into a larger or smaller circle just by moving up or down in the plane of Flatland. It can even disappear entirely by rising above or sinking below this plane. The sphere tries and tries to explain to the square the idea of having thickness as well as height and breadth, but the square simply can't grasp the idea of being above or below the universe it inhabits. The square is quite sophisticated in its grasp of two-dimensional geometry, and the sphere tries to explain the concept by using analogies the square could understand such as the difference between one dimension and two and how a third dimension is simply a progression of this idea. However, the square persists in calling the entire concept ridiculous.

Finally the sphere, in a moment of frustration, grabs the square and jerks it up above Flatland so it can look down on the world and see it in its entirety. Now able to see inside and outside of all the other characters and all it had ever known, the square reacts in this way:

"An unspeakable horror seized me. There was darkness, then a dizzy, sickening sensation of sight that was not like seeing. I saw space that was not space. I was myself and not myself. When I could find voice, I shrieked aloud in agony. 'Either this is madness or it is hell.' 'It is neither,' calmly replied the sphere. 'It is knowledge; it is three dimensions; open your eyes and try to look steadily.' I looked, and behold, a new world!"

The square is transfixed. This vision profoundly and permanently affects the square and turns its world inside out. It falls down before the sphere in reverent awe and becomes a disciple. When it returns to Flatland, it begins to preach this "Gospel of Three Dimensions." No one understands what it is talking about, and they label the square a fool.[ccc]

Hasn't everybody had an experience at some time like that of the square—an experience of transport out of the mundane, two-dimensional parameters that define ordinary, day-to-day existence? Perhaps it was an experience of nature and its great wonders. Maybe it was a moment of great beauty or great emotion when one could completely lose oneself and the petty concerns that ordinarily define the world we inhabit. Perhaps it was the unmistakable presence of something larger than humanity—something possibly called the divine or God. Perhaps the spirit was uplifted in a sublime way. Perhaps the experience eclipsed anything in the known world, and the observer found he or she was not poet enough to describe it with any words or symbols of common parlance.

Johnathan Haidt, author of *The Happiness Hypothesis*, connects Flatland to the relational dimensions of ordinary lives. He says one of these is the dimension of closeness such as among friends and family. People situate themselves along this axis in relation to others depending on whether the other is a stranger, acquaintance, or a close friend or relative. People codify this distance or closeness in ways such as direct address. Strangers are greeted as Mr. Smith or Ms. Jones. Acquaintances are greeted by their first names, and close friends or relations are given pet names or nicknames. The second dimension is hierarchy—the distinctions people give to others as they understand their relative positions in an intricate, complex societal chain of command. For instance, people give titles to politicians such as Judge Brown or Senator Byrd. People address a police officer as "officer" and a minister as "reverend." A superior is called "mister" or "miss," and subordinates are called by their first names. A customer is called "sir" or "ma'am," and people are encouraged to call salespeople by their first names through a system of name tags. We move about in these two dimensions fairly freely, and our minds automatically keep track of these fairly complex ties and affiliations.

Haidt connects the extraordinary third dimension of the story to the divine. Haidt, who calls himself a Jewish atheist, chose this label for the third dimension because his extensive research into human psychology and morality indicated the human mind perceived a dimension of divinity and sacredness regardless of God's perceived existence. He believes that losing sight of this dimension and collapsing our world into two dimensions leads to impoverishment of human existence. He also believes any effort to impose a specific view of this third dimension is the hallmark of religious fundamentalism.[DDD]

The aim of any religion's beliefs and practices has always been to move up and out of the profane two-dimensional world into the sacred third dimension. The founders of the great religious traditions were those remarkable individuals who escaped this plane of existence, and once they returned they managed to maintain the vision and (unlike the square in the story) successfully communicated it to others. Religious communities grew up around them, and the community members, quite predictably, came to articulate the vision using similar symbols and language. This gave the community remarkable cohesiveness and sustainability, but it all but excluded anyone who did not adopt the common language and phraseology. Since these remarkable individuals who had these grand experiences each took unique trajectories away from the plane of ordinary secular life, each of their religion's litanies, rituals, and sacred writings had its own particular character. Over time, though, each community's unique practices became increasingly a part of the ordinary dimensions of that religious community. Once again there was a need for a prophetic "sphere" from that third dimension to come along and revitalize it. Often the community does not accept the words of this prophetic person, and the prophet or prophetess wanders off to join another community on another trajectory. He or she might even start a new one.

The story of Flatland helped me make some sense of many aspects of my spiritual journey, especially the community-building workshop I referred to in chapter nine. Like the square in Flatland, being pulled out of my ordinary two dimensional world by that experience of community profoundly and permanently affected me and turned my world inside out. Our facilitators at the workshop were aware that the experience is profound and disorienting to many and prepared us as best they could. With our facilitators help, every person in that group was eventually able to transcend the two-dimensional perspective of his or her previous world view, join in the awesome vision, and be a part of something totally new. That something new was the creation of the the unique community made up of fifty-three remarkable, courageous individuals who took the risks necessary to reach escape velocity from the "Flatland" of ordinary life.

The parallels of the community building experience to those of the square extended to what we experienced on reentry to the real world also. Just as the square wanted to worship the sphere and preach the gospel of three dimensions, when the workshop participants returned home we wanted to tell everyone about it and insist others should come and experience community also. The facilitators warned us not to try to proselytize others with community building, but when I returned from the workshop, I had to preach the "gospel" of community to everyone around me until I managed to alienate a critical mass of my friends and family. After a few years, I managed to reach a level of maturity and acceptance so I could just live the vision and not try to gain converts. As I look back, though, the really significant thing that happened was that I was no longer at home in my previous religious perspective. I was no longer comfortable in the church I had been attending. The people in that conference room came from all sorts of religions; many claimed no religion at all. That I could bond with them and see divinity within them made no sense in the language and messages my church community insisted was the truth. My experience taught me something different, and I had to move on. I needed a religious home where people desired to transcend the two-dimensional plane of ordinary life but without the compulsion to gain that sacred dimension by way of a predetermined path. This led to my gravitation toward Universalism. In my vision of that third dimension, people from many different paths (even those on diametrically opposed paths) had all gained a place of spiritual oneness. I now held a deep conviction there were many different trajectories leading to this sacred dimension I so longed to inhabit. I would, therefore, need a religious community where that sort of vision was possible.

This is how I have come to understand and attempt to explain the sacred dimension of my life. However, I am still like the two-dimensional square before enlightenment, and I always will be. It comes with the territory of being human. It is impossible for humans to come up with an adequate way to describe or explain things larger than ourselves. Take electricity, for instance. An electrician might be able to explain it using diagrams of circuits that carry current from the power plant to the outlet in the wall to the device I want to plug in. My son, the electrical engineer, might be able to explain it as the flow of electrons excited in a generator to line up and pass along various copper wires into the motor or semiconductor of my appliance. Who can really say what electricity is, though? Humans might come to know certain laws of physics and mechanical rules that govern its behavior, but at its heart it is still very much a mystery. Divinity, God, or whatever name given to the sacred dimension of life (if a name is necessary at all) is also like that. The most anyone can say about it is from personal experience. Some have the ability to do that more articulately and convincingly, but to do any more than that is the reason there is so much misunderstanding, strife, and hatred around the issue of religious faith. Given that humans lack a language or common frame of reference to describe such glimpses of this sacred dimension, tensions and divisions will likely continue to plague efforts to create a more tolerant and ecumenical world. However, if people understand a little more about why it is this way, perhaps they can make religion a little less divisive.

It seems to works something like this. In the disorientation that likely follows a profound transcendent experience, where is a religious person likely to turn other than to traditional religious language? That strong human tendency is equally matched by an equally strong (though opposite) one. Those who have been put off by the religious conventions of the church, temple, or synagogue of their formative years are likely to resort to a smug conceit against that religious institution's words and phrases once they experience something that completely transcends anything they ever felt or experienced there. So they will search diligently for other ways to express themselves. Is it any wonder, given the profound differences in religious orientations, that such profound ecstatic experiences would be so divisive?

These powerful forces within the human psyche are unleashed during momentary visits to this third dimension, and they can have a myriad of effects on human lives. Fortunately the fervent passions often unleashed in this "sacred" third dimension can remain with the individual and can lead them to be more loving and compassionate. Unfortunately they can also result in derision, animosity, or even violence when the mind constellates the experience around some exclusive fundamentalist interpretation. In full knowledge I am speaking from the perspective of just another two-dimensional square, I end this chapter with a story from the Indian saint Ramakrishna, who led many people into the third dimension.

A woman told Ramakrishna, "I find I do not love God. The concept does not move me."

Ramakrishna asked her, "Is there nothing in the world you do love?"

She said, "Yes. I love my little nephew."

He said, "There God is—in your love for that nephew."[EEE]

May we all find the grace to create safe spaces for others to speak of their experiences with whatever words and in whatever language they can best express themselves. May we also have the courage and fortitude to speak of our own sacred experiences in such a way they might translate into a blessing for those who listen.

* * *

twenty

What If God Was One of Us?

It was a particularly cold evening one December a few years ago when my wife, Kathy, and I got the call. Her Uncle Burt was in jail. He had been picked up for driving while intoxicated. This was no surprise to us. Burt was a known alcoholic and had a long history of trouble with the law because of it. This was him calling and asking us to come down to the local jail in the small town where we were living and bail him out. This part was a first for us. In the past he usually called one of his sisters or one of his kids to help him when he got in trouble or down on his luck. However, he had burned his bridges with most of his other relatives over the years, and now he was turning to us. Kathy answered the phone and talked to him for a few minutes. After she hung up, she asked me what I thought we should do. We talked about it for a few minutes and came to the decision we would go down to the jail and see him. We would only get him out of jail, though, if he agreed to go immediately to the alcohol detox center in a city some sixty miles away.

When we arrived at the jail, Burt's wife, Betty, greeted us. She was also an alcoholic and had been drinking rather heavily that evening. Since she had not been driving, she was not arrested. The three of us were allowed to visit Burt. Burt remained very quiet as Kathy and I told him what we were willing to do. We knew from experience that Burt could be stubborn and defensive, especially when intoxicated, and he told us in no uncertain terms that he was not going to the detox center. Betty pleaded with him to go and said she was willing to go herself. Burt would not be persuaded. So we called the jailer, and he took Burt back to his cell.

Betty, however, remained humble and contrite, and she pleaded with us to take her to detox. I was on call for the hospital where I worked and could not leave town, but Kathy agreed to take her. I wasn't crazy about the idea of Kathy going on the road that late at night with a drunk in tow, but there didn't seem to be a better plan. We didn't want to leave Betty alone, and there was nothing else we could do with her. So Kathy dropped me off at our house, and then she took off with Betty for the detox center.

By the time Kathy arrived in the city it was raining heavily. Kathy had no idea where the detox center was, and Betty was no help. Kathy stopped at a convenience store and asked directions, but the person who gave her directions apparently had no idea where the detox center was either because the directions got Kathy lost. By this time Betty had passed out on the seat beside her. This was actually a blessing because all Betty could do in her drunken stupor was cry and attempt to help Kathy drive. After asking several people for directions and following them, Kathy ended up not at detox but at the AA meeting house. It was really getting late now, and Kathy was a bit shaken by everything. There was still a light on in the AA building but only one car left in the parking lot. Kathy knew she was in the wrong place, but she also knew that if anyone in town knew where the center was, she would probably find that person here. She got her umbrella out and went in to ask. The light went out in the building as she approached the door. Its last occupant was headed toward his car. Kathy called out to him.

He came over to her car. He looked in the car window and saw Betty's condition. Through the desperation in Kathy's voice, this stranger quickly surmised the situation and said he would be glad to help. There was something about this stranger that engendered Kathy's trust. She even allowed him to get in the car with her and direct her to detox. Once there he helped her fill out Betty's admission papers. Betty had nothing with her except the clothes on her back, and the staff at the detox center told Kathy that Betty would need a few personal items to get her through the next few days. This stranger again said he would help and accompanied Kathy to a convenience store to pick these items up. Then he went back to detox with Kathy and helped get Betty settled in. Then Kathy took the stranger back to AA and his car. He was a good listener and allowed Kathy to vent all her fears and frustrations as they drove.

When they got back to AA, Kathy thanked the man profusely for all his help, and she confessed she would not have been able to make it through this ordeal without him. Then it dawned on her. Even though this man had introduced himself when they first met, with all that was going on, she had not made a mental note of his name. Kathy said, "Excuse me, but with all that's happened tonight, I have forgotten your name. Could you please tell me again?"

With a smile, he said, "Ma'am, my name is easy to remember. It's Love. Ben Love." With that he disappeared into the night.

Kathy's experience with Ben Love was reminiscent of a television show that appeared briefly in 2003 called *Joan of Arcadia*. It was about a teenage girl whom God visited on a recurring basis as she went about her daily life. Through Joan God intervened for good in the affairs of the people around her. What made the show intriguing was that God appeared to Joan in and through the ordinary people she met along her way. The theme song of the show was "One of Us" by Joan Osborne. The lyrics spoke to the message of the show:

> "What if God was one of us?
> Just a slob like one of us?
> Just a stranger on the bus
> Trying to make his way home."[FFF]

Joan of Arcadia was on the air when Kathy took Betty to rehab and met Ben Love. The incident made us think of the show. Kathy swears, just like Joan of Arcadia, she met God that cold, rainy night—or at least one of God's angels. Who could disagree with Kathy's assessment? Almost as if by divine intervention, someone appeared to her in an hour of need. Even all these years later, I still get goose bumps just thinking about it.

What if God were one of us? (If the word "God" doesn't speak to you, then substitute divinity. What if there is something of the divine in a human being? Think about this distinction for a moment—divine versus human. What's that about? Apparently it's important because people have been arguing and even killing each other over it for thousands of years. How did this state of affairs come about?

Since the beginning, in the process of trying to understand the world, we pitiful humans have used words to compartmentalize things. We have made the universe dualistic. Everything is understood in terms of its opposite—light and darkness, male and female, life and death, good and evil, true and untrue, divine and human, and more. This is useful up to a point. In some ways conversations and even thought itself would not be possible without compartmentalization and categorization. Problems arise, however, in these distinctions. This is especially true with ethereal things such as "God."

Humans ate of the tree of knowledge in the Garden of Eden. This is a mythological story to explain what I just discussed in psychological terms—why humans think dualistically. We entered the field of time, we learned to think in opposites, and we gained much in the process. We also lost much, though. Thinking dualistically means losing that sense of oneness both with the universe and with each other. Adam and Eve were kicked out of the Garden—the Garden of holistic, nondualistic thinking.

So how do humans put the universe back together? Theologians have tried to help. Unfortunately they often use complex words such as "incarnation" that often leave people only more confused. Theologians often make incarnation more complex than it need be. Incarnation is the idea that God could appear to us in the flesh as a real, live human being—able to touch and be touched. That is a beautiful, simple idea when taken in its raw form without all the accumulated ideas built around it over the past two millennia and the additional baggage the church has piled onto it. Incarnation. Emmanuel. God with us. That's what we're supposed to mean when we sing the Christmas carol, "O Come, Emmanuel." Come be with us, God. Be one of us.

My life has been a series of experiences that suggest the idea of incarnation got messy and caused all sorts of problems when the church made God's appearance an exclusive. When it insisted the Jesus event was a onetime deal for God. The church claimed dibs on incarnation and the Jesus event closed out God's personal appearances on the stage of history. It claimed Jesus was the one and only time the metaphysical creator of the universe would get down off his high horse and do a gig as a flesh and blood human being.

How absurd. Why did the idea have to be cordoned off to only apply to Jesus? Why is it that the word "divine" can only apply to God, Jesus, and something called the Holy Spirit, and the rest of us are just "human?"

The musical question Joan Osborne asked, the question *Joan of Arcadia* asked, and the mystery Kathy actually experienced is, why does the idea of God and the divine have to be so limited? What if God was one of us?

The Christmas story, as recorded in the Gospel of Luke, is about a baby being born in a stable. The baby becomes known as the Messiah. "Messiah" can be variously understood as deliverer, savior, or even God. What might have been the original intent of this story? Doesn't it make sense that the original storyteller was simply conveying the message that God was to become one of us?

It's not necessary to know a lot about the historical and cultural setting of first-century Palestine to recognize that, according to the story, the Messiah made an appearance in the most unlikely of circumstances. He was born to an unwed teen with no place to stay but among the animals in a barn. Yet the world has come to understand this as an appearance of the divine. Such is the power of story and myth. If they only allowed it, the story could challenge people to ask themselves, "Can it not be so in our day as well?"

What if God was one of us?

* * *

twenty one

God and Civility

An essay called "Why I Raise My Children Without God" appeared on CNN's iReport on January 14, 2013. Within four days, it had over 650,000 hits. It obviously struck a chord. The essay begins:

"When my son was around three years old, he used to ask me a lot of questions about heaven. Where is it? How do people walk without a body? How will I find you? You know the questions that kids ask.

For over a year, I lied to him and made up stories that I didn't believe about heaven. Like most parents, I love my child so much that I didn't want him to be scared. I wanted him to feel safe and loved and full of hope. But the trade-off was that I would have to make stuff up, and I would have to brainwash him into believing stories that didn't make sense, stories that I didn't believe either."[GGG]

Deborah Mitchell is the mother of two teens and the author of the essay. She wrote it because, "I just felt there is not a voice out there for women/moms like me. I think people misunderstand or are fearful of people who don't believe in God."[HHH] In the interest of fairness and balance, CNN also published a rebuttal essay from a parent called "Why I Raise My Children with God."

Deborah's essay had a profound effect on me. It is remarkable both because of the articulate way it's written and because of the courage it took this mother to post something that was bound to generate passionate responses. I also commend CNN for posting it and moderating the generated conversation in a way that has allowed it to be passionate and mostly civil. After her post ran on CNN, Mitchell said she was encouraged by the number of people who agreed with her or who disagreed but wanted to have respectful conversations.

I was drawn to this online conversation. I think it's important, even though I don't think a single one of those 650,000 people will change his or her mind on the issue of God based on Mitchell's essay or the rebuttal essay. The theist versus nontheist debate has really worn thin on the religious sensibilities of a postmodern world. This debate has been going on for decades within Unitarian Universalist churches, and nobody has gained anything from it. Regardless of which side one's opinion falls on in the debate, everyone loses. People have left churches in droves in the aftermath of the animosity generated by the debate. When all's said and done, it doesn't seem that having the right opinion on God matters—whatever that "right" opinion is. Religious faith is about something much deeper than our opinions or beliefs. (see Part II on Faith)

So what does matter? What matters is civility in the way people treat those with differing ideas or beliefs. What matters is that people are able to express themselves freely and to use the words and language they feel they need to use to tell their stories. Some need to use the word "God." Some need to react against that word to tell the emotionally significant narrative of their lives. The idea of God is critical for the spiritual growth of some. For others the idea of God is a detriment to spiritual development. Unless people are able to live in the tension of this paradox, they are destined to merely add to the misunderstanding, confusion, and mistrust that surrounds and haunts the world when it comes to religion.

Belief in God is a paradoxical, multidimensional issue in regards to human psychological and spiritual development. Take Jesus and the way he spoke of God. Jesus called God "Abba"—a word translated as "father" but actually meaning something closer to "daddy." For Jesus religious faith was about having a personal relationship with God, and the metaphor of the relationship between a loving daddy and his child served Jesus well in getting the message of his teachings across to his followers. The idea of a personal God (God as a loving daddy) was revolutionary at that time. Jesus portrayed God as relational, intimate, personally interested in humans, numbering the hairs on our heads, and seeing us of more value than many sparrows. There has never been a better press agent for God than Jesus. The image Jesus created of God as the heavenly father was wildly appealing and likely partly explains the exponential growth of Christianity in those early years.

What if this metaphor doesn't work for you, though? What if your father was not a kind, gentle, loving daddy? What if he abused you verbally, emotionally, physically, or even sexually? Then what? If your relationship with your father brings up painful memories, then so too will any notion of God as a heavenly father. For some, consciously or subconsciously, this imagery of God does not create feelings of love and protection. It only strikes terror in the heart. It's not healthy, comforting, or conducive to spiritual growth and well-being. In the Bible Belt where I live, the culture insists on referring to God as masculine. God is the father. Is it any wonder the idea of God would become problematic for so many?

This is just one example of innumerable problems encountered when the word "God" enters the common discourse. God as father calls up a certain imagery and, powerful though that imagery is, may or may not be edifying for every person. It illustrates in psychological terms why the word can evoke such passionate responses. "God" is an emotionally charged word.

It also carries a ton of intellectual baggage. No one can logically prove the existence of God. Neither can anyone prove God doesn't exist. Whenever the word is used, it evokes a mystery—the mystery of the universe, life, and us. God is a mystery. It is a mystery no matter how vehemently the fundamentalists insist they have the issue nailed down by a fixed set of premises. I'm speaking of fundamentalists of both the Bible-thumping and atheistic varieties. Yes, atheism has a fundamentalist segment as well. Witness the dogmatism of the Sam Harrises, Richard Dawkinses, and Christopher Hitchenses of the world.

The author and psychiatrist Scott Peck did a lot of thinking in this area, and in his book *The Road Less Traveled,* he makes a forceful and persuasive case that belief in God can be either beneficial or detrimental to psychological and spiritual health. He claims it depends on where the person is psychologically and spiritually. Peck begins with the rhetorical questions, "Is belief in God a sickness? Is such a belief a form of primitive or childish thinking which we should grow out of as we seek higher levels of awareness and maturity? It is tempting to think that humanity might be better off without a belief in God, that God is not only pie in the sky by and by, but a poisoned pie at that. It would seem reasonable to conclude that God is an illusion in the minds of humans—a destructive illusion—and that belief in God is a common form of human psychopathology that should be healed."[III]

Peck then examines in-depth the question of belief in God as a sickness. He uses the case histories of three patients—Kathy, Marcia, and Ted. Peck demonstrates clearly, I think, that the answer is yes. And no.

The first patient, Kathy, was the victim of a domineering mother who instilled in her from an early age an unhealthy concept of God as a sort of puritanical tyrant. Her mother used this image of God to cement her parental authority, and Kathy never developed the capacity to function autonomously. She led her life in the shadow of a tyrannical God who was ready to extract a pound of flesh for any activity that might be construed as a sin. So as Kathy grew up, she began to avoid people, places, and situations that would lead to any activity that might lead her to sin. She began to pray in ritualistic ways to avoid sexual thoughts. Her prayer rituals evolved into chants. Kathy's world became narrower and narrower. Her inner life spiraled as she became increasingly obsessed with these chants. Eventually she ended up in a psychiatric hospital, huddled in a corner, and chanting to herself. It was only through painstaking work with Peck over several months that Kathy learned how to think for herself and develop a healthy skepticism about the things her mother and culture had taught her about morality. Only when Kathy ditched her ideas of God was she able to grow and develop psychologically and spiritually and become her own person.

The second patient, Marcia, suffered from a condition called anhedonia. Her life, though appearing stable outwardly, was quite joyless. She took no delight in work or relationships, and she had little in the way of outside interests or hobbies. When she began therapy with Peck, she proclaimed herself a staunch atheist. The source of her anhedonia stemmed from her upbringing in a household where her parents provided for her physically but were totally invested in their careers and were always emotionally distant. In her formative years, Marcia never knew what it was to feel warmth and closeness, and this lack of significant emotional ties stunted her ability to generate passion for anything. During the course of therapy, Marcia learned the value of human relationships, and as she did, her rigid, scornful views of religion and God also began to soften.

The third patient, Ted, came to see Peck because, though intelligent, he seemed to lack any focus or ambition, and he felt he was wasting his life. It was discovered that his family had made his life miserable by taking away anything he showed any enthusiasm for. Combined with the tragic loss of his best friend at an early age, he undertook a self-imposed exile in a cabin in the woods. Through therapy Peck uncovered the deep but largely subconscious resentment Ted had developed toward life and by extension toward God—as Ted understood God. However, Ted's attitude toward God was inconsistent. He tended to blame God for the bad things in his life, but when something good happened, he would only credit it to luck. Once Ted worked through his feelings toward his family for their emotional abuse, he saw the inconsistency in his feelings about God, and his belief system began to change. Subsequently Ted came to the decision that the best way to express his newfound enthusiasm for life was to go into the ministry.[JJJ]

Three patients. Three different beliefs about God. One began with an unquestioning belief in God and ended up discarding this belief. A second began as an atheist and in due course started to entertain the possibility that God might make for a brighter, more optimistic outlook on life. A third started out being rather snobbish about religion, considering anyone who believed in God beneath him, and finally emerged from therapy with a desire to pursue the ministry.

Is belief in God healthy? Is it healthy to teach to children? The answer would seem to be yes. And no. What are people to do with this seeming paradox? The stories of these patients would suggest it is possible (even necessary) to mature out of a belief in God. They also suggest it is possible (even healthy) for the skeptic to mature into a belief in God. In Peck's words, "A skeptical atheism or agnosticism is not necessarily the highest state of understanding at which human beings can arrive."[KKK]

In conclusion I would just say humans do a disservice to themselves and their ability to grow and relate to others if they have fixed perceptions about God and dogmatically cling to beliefs. Not all beliefs are good or healthy. To nurture personal spiritual growth, humans need to recognize that the use of the word "God" is a part of the everyday parlance of the vast majority of people. People need to learn the fine and courageous art of being conversational, maintaining identity, and holding convictions while still making room for others to tell their stories using the language they choose.

I can express it no better than Deborah Mitchell did at the end of her essay. "I'm not saying that everybody should think how I do. I'm saying the people that do should have a place in our society and have acceptance and respect," she said. "I just want to have children grow up and be able to not be afraid to say, 'I don't believe that,' or 'I'm not part of that.'"[LLL]

May we find the courage and cultivate the ability to make it so in our relationships and with those we encounter in this world.

* * *

twenty two

Meeting in Rumi's Field

The following is a short story called "Building Bridges."

Once upon a time, a missionary team established a church in a remote village in Africa. After constructing a church building, the missionaries set out upon their main task, which was to build a bridge across the river that separated the village from the road system of the country. The completed bridge would give the isolated village land access to nearby towns and cities.

Brother Zach was the leader of the missionary team. Besides his role as chief engineer for the bridge project, he also preached every Sunday. Everyone who knew Brother Zach said he was a devoted man of God.

Each day it was Brother Zach's practice to spend some time walking around the village. He observed the ways of the native people and conversed with them. Like most missionaries Brother Zach lived in hope of finding some way to convey his faith to the local native people. Through much effort he had become conversational in their language. The natives came to know and like Brother Zach. Even though they were quite shy by nature, they would welcome his visits and go out of their way to talk to him.

Though he was diligent in his efforts to get to know them and become a part of the community, there was little interest among the natives in attending the church. Even after three years, attendance at the church consisted mostly of the missionary team. Occasionally a few native women would come and sit in the back pew but never any of the men. Sometimes a much larger group would gather under the trees around the church, and some of the men would even climb the trees to see in the windows. One Sunday Brother Zach had saw the tribal chief in the group. They seemed to be attracted to the music and singing, and he had even heard some of them trying to sing the hymns down in the village on occasion. If he went outside and invited the natives into the church, though, they only ran away.

The missionaries only vaguely understood the folk religion of the natives. Often the missionaries would hear chanting and drum-beating into the night, and they came to understand that these events were religious ceremonies. Brother Zach never questioned the natives about these events. He reasoned that the natives might resent him for prying.

One evening after his customary visit into the village, he noticed the locals scurrying to the hillside where these ceremonies were conducted. A somewhat out-of-character thought came to him. "I'll go and discreetly observe one of their rituals to see if I can understand these people better. Then maybe I'll know how to talk with them about God." So he slipped through the underbrush and climbed a tree just behind their site where several of them were building a fire. For what seemed like an eternity to his weary arms, he watched the proceedings. The natives adorned their bodies with colorful costumes and face paint. There was music, chanting, and dancing. It was all rather odd to him, but there wasn't anything in their practices that offended him, and he didn't think any of it would give offense to his missionary group either. He was quite thankful about this.

When the event seemed to be drawing to a close, he began to climb down. He was glad he had learned what he had and that he had not been discovered. Suddenly the branch where his foot rested gave way, and he came crashing down out of the tree. The clamor of his fall startled the natives, and all the drums and chanting were silenced. In a few moments, they began to cautiously approach the site where Brother Zach lay writhing in pain. (Later the doctor in the missionary group diagnosed him with a severely sprained ankle.) As the natives approached, Brother Zach's pain gave way to fear. He wondered what terrible fate awaited someone caught spying on their ceremonies. His terror soon melted away when the faces looking down at him smiled, and he recognized several grins behind the face paint. The native chief now approached. Brother Zach followed the chief's gaze up into the tree and then down to his ankle, and the half smile that came over the chief's face revealed to Brother Zach that the chief had figured out what he had been doing and even the motivation behind Brother Zach's clandestine activity. At this point the chief instructed the natives to carry him into the clearing. Then he ordered all but one to depart, and this one he told to go get the missionaries.

Once they were alone, Brother Zach was quick to offer an apology for his intrusion. The chief rebuked him by mention of his own presence outside the church. Brother Zach then inquired about the ceremony he had just witnessed. As the chief explained, he listened attentively. As best Brother Zach could surmise across the cultural divide, the natives did worship a god of some sort.

As he began to feel more relaxed with the chief, Brother Zach brought up his church and his desire to have the natives come one Sunday. The chief responded to him, "Did you not come here tonight to learn more about us and more about our God?"

Zach did not know how to respond. He stammered. "No." Then, a reluctant, "Well, perhaps. I guess so."

The chief said nothing for a time, smiled, and then said, "You and I are not so different. Perhaps I will see you Sunday."

Sunday came. Brother Zach's ankle didn't hurt so much now. The chief came, and so did several of the native families. The service went well.

After the service Zach thanked the chief for coming. Before they parted his inquisitiveness overcame him again, and he asked the chief, "What is the difference now? Why was it OK to come now?"

The chief replied, "I didn't understand you and your religion before. But the man that was in the treetop at our campfire—he is a man I understand. He doesn't have all the answers. He has a heart that remains open."

It seems to be part and parcel of human nature to think we have it right about God. That we've got dibs on the truth. Whether one subscribes to the idea there is a God (theism) or there isn't a God (atheism), or whether one openly admits one doesn't know (agnosticism) or care (apatheism), it just seems to go with the territory to think one holds the superior position, and anyone whose opinion differs is suffering from some form of self-delusion. In society groups also have this tendency and people tend to congregate with others whose ideas about God approximate their own. Therefore, there are situations in towns and cities all over the country, in countless different churches, each thinking its theology, knowledge of the divine being, and thinking about God is the one and only right way. What a strange way for society to arrange itself. Especially when considering no one really knows about God. Whether one's faith is to believe in God or not, it's all done on faith. It's all a mystery.

God as a mystery is actually quite a useful idea. The idea of God as the perennial mystery fosters a kind of humility that seems sorely lacking among many religious people today. In the mythic story of Moses before the burning bush, Moses hears a voice calling out to him. When Moses asks who is speaking, God answers, "I am who

I am." This was later shortened to YHWH, or Yahweh. Mysterious. Ineffable. Joseph Campbell said this about God, "God is a thought. God is a name. God is an idea. But its reference is to something that transcends all thinking. The ultimate mystery of being is beyond all categories of thought."[MMM] It would seem right thinking on the idea of God just isn't possible. Yet here we are living in a world where so many uphold their own brands of religious truth as exclusively right.

Rumi, the thirteenth-century poet and Sufi mystic, had a saying. "Out beyond right thinking and wrong thinking there is a field. I will meet you there."

As I thought about Rumi's field, the story about Brother Zach came to me. The story speaks of two men who found themselves in Rumi's field quite by accident. It took an unexpected fall to bring it about. Nonetheless, they ended up meeting in a sacred space that seemed somewhat reminiscent of Rumi's field—a place that compelled them beyond the right thinking and wrong thinking they used to categorize each other's views of God and religion. Because circumstances threw them together in such a way, they ended up in a place where they could laugh at themselves and their own curious natures—a place where their ideas of God dissolved into an experience of God within and beyond each other and the limits of "thinking."

Meeting in Rumi's field is not confined to fiction. Though unfortunately rare, it can happen in real life also. As in this true story from my own life.

I remember this story well because it was one of those moments that set me on a slightly different path. It was an event that helped shape me in a small but very significant way. I remember the story because it's a memory that allows me to use the word "God" today without reservation. This event occurred some forty years ago when I was in college at Valdosta State.

Bobby and I met in the weight room of all places. It was my junior year of college. In addition to the intellectual discoveries I was making, I was also discovering girls, and I wanted to develop all these muscles to impress them. Bobby and I stayed in the same dorm, worked out together, and ate at the cafeteria together. Occasionally I would even go with him to his little hometown church in Clyattville, which was near Valdosta.

I'm sure Bobby and I were an odd sight walking across campus. I was tall and skinny, and Bobby short and broad shouldered. I was all gangly and socially awkward. He was all muscle and quiet contemplation. He was the sort that deserved the nickname "Stump."

Bobby and I liked to talk about life, ideas, religion, and philosophy. One day, though, we were sitting in the cafeteria after church having one of our conversations, and a question came to my mind that demanded an honest answer. Bobby and I had long past the point we felt it necessary to use traditional Christian jargon when we conversed, but I was about to push our dialogue to a whole new level of frankness and integrity. I asked Bobby about the Bible. Specifically I asked him, "Do you think this Book is exactly, word for word, the whole truth?"

I had asked this question to other Christians before, but before I always got a pat answer or a blank stare. This time I sat there in Bobby's prolonged quiet reverie as he contemplated his response. I began to anticipate that his answer would be profound. Little did I know the answer would be one of the shaping moments of my life.

He said, "Well, I know too much not to believe in a God of some sort, and it makes sense to me that if there is a God, he would want to communicate with his creation in some way. Now it might not be exactly word for word correct, but I believe his basic message is in there."

I ask you to look past Bobby's exclusive use of the male pronoun for God, and consider the substance of what he said to me that day.

Up until that day and for many years afterward, this was the only time I ever felt another human being was being totally honest with me about his or her faith. Bobby had answered my question openly and honestly from the depths of his being—no joking put-downs, no dogma, and no pat answers. It was just an answer based on simple existential reasoning. It was an answer anyone could understand and appreciate whether that person agreed or not.

His answer really wasn't all that novel. I had reasoned it out for myself and had come to a somewhat similar conclusion. Though, I wouldn't have expressed it quite the way he did. However, the really crucial thing, the aspect of this encounter that gave it its gravitas, was that Bobby spoke from a place beyond all the answers he had ever been taught or told were right or wrong. By doing that he was acknowledging the validity of my question and affirming me for mustering the courage to even ask. The courage, honesty, and integrity of his answer created a connection between us. I didn't fully understand what had happened in that moment of connection, and I don't fully understand it even today. However, when I first heard Rumi's quote, my thoughts immediately went to this incident long ago, and I realized Bobby and I had met in Rumi's field.

There are ways to learn to meet others in Rumi's field. It doesn't have to happen by accident as it did for Brother Zach and the tribal chief or in some freewheeling bull session as it did for Bobby and me. There are ways to live life and be present to others that foster encounters in sacred space such as Rumi's field.

The Jewish philosopher Martin Buber wrote a wonderful book called *I and Thou* in which he describes this sacred space. "Our relationship lives in the space between us—it doesn't live in me or in you or even in the dialogue between the two us—it lives in the space we live together and that space is sacred space."[NNN]

There is a profound usefulness in envisioning relationships in this way (as existing in a sacred space created between the participants). It's useful because once one realizes it is sacred space, one becomes more conscious of all the ways people consciously or subconsciously contaminate that space. Even the simplest of things can contaminate it. That includes a word, a gesture, or even an inflection of the voice. Sometimes it's a word that has a different meaning for both people. Sometimes it's an emotion that the other person is not ready for. Yes. Everyone has a right to have feelings, and feelings are important. However, when people put that intensity into this space at inappropriate times or in inappropriate ways, it can contaminate that sacred space. People also contaminate this space when they hold too tightly to the names and labels they give themselves. Labels such as "Christian," "atheist," "Unitarian," "Universalist," "liberal," or "conservative." These names might have very different meanings and connotations for the other person, and that might spark fear and defensiveness.

There are ways to make the path to Rumi's field—to this sacred space—more accessible. They are the principles of community building, and it is the purpose of a community of faith to live and teach these rules.

* * *

Part V

Christianity

twenty three

Finding Spiritual Treasure

Once there lived in Kraków a pious rabbi named Eisik. He was very poor. One night as he slept on the dirt floor of his hovel, he had a dream that told him to go to Prague, and there under the bridge that led to the royal castle he could unearth a great treasure. The dream was repeated a second night and a third.

He decided to set out for Prague. After many days walking, he entered Prague, and he found the bridge that led to the royal castle. However, he could not dig. The bridge was guarded day and night. The rabbi walked back and forth awaiting a moment when the bridge might be unwatched and he could dig for the treasure. The captain of the guard noticed him and went up to him. "I've noticed you walking around here these several days. Have you lost something?" At this the rabbi innocently narrated his tale. "Really?" said the captain of the guard. He was a secular, modern man and unconnected with his dreams. "Have you worn out all your shoe leather merely on account of a dream? I too have had a dream, three times. It told me to go to the town of Kraków, look for the Rabbi Eisik, and dig in his dirt floor behind his stove in the middle of his room. There I would find a great treasure. But dreams are silly superstitions."

The rabbi immediately understood and promptly returned home. He entered his hovel and dug underneath the heart of his hearth where the warmth of his own being lay. There he unearthed a treasure that put an end to his poverty.°°°

This Hasidic tale speaks a simple spiritual truth. A spiritual journey ultimately leads back to the person and to his or her own innermost being. However, it is a lesson that continually needs to be brought to people's attention because something in the human spirit seems to resist the teaching.

This story resonates with me as I reflect on my own religious past and where I am now in my pilgrimage. My spiritual meanderings began because of the deprivation I keenly sensed in the stiff, formal Presbyterian church of my childhood. I dreamed of a place where all the big questions about the life of the soul didn't have pat answers out of a catechism. I took refuge among the Baptists for a time. They didn't have creeds or a catechism and talked a lot about the priesthood of all believers. They also said all people had the freedom to interpret the Bible for themselves. However, it gradually became evident there were limits to this freedom, and it didn't extend to a place where it was safe to ask many of the questions I had as my faith was developing.

While among the Baptists, though, I did learn how most people confuse faith with certainty. When a group believes something with complete conviction, then the matter is completely settled for them. They stop taking in information. Faith equals certainty, and anyone who questions that certainty is annoying or possibly even dangerous. An insatiably curious person about the life of the soul is probably not going to find a religious home anywhere other than a Unitarian Universalist church, and that is why I eventually wandered to that faith community.

The real application of the story for me, though, is that my search for treasure eventually led me back home to myself and my own religious tradition. Though I consider myself a Unitarian Universalist, I never abandoned Christianity. I had my doubts, and I still do, but no longer do I consider them evidence of a lack of faith. Now I am able to see my doubts as elements of my faith. I am still curious and still open to taking in new ideas and new information about other religions and faith traditions. I still want to learn about all the different ways people approach the sacred dimension of life.

There have been many people along the path of my spiritual journey who have functioned as the captain of the guard did for Rabbi Eisik. They directed me back to myself and the religious tradition of my formative years. One stands out, though, as giving me the critical tool that enabled me to go back home and dig in the right place and in the right way to unearth the treasure that was there all along. That person was the mythologist Joseph Campbell.

Campbell talked about his years of teaching comparative mythology at Sarah Lawrence College and how he would be comparing the images and stories of one religious system with another. This would often help give clarity and meaning to some aspect of the other. Some symbol or ritual that had previously been seen as strange, mysterious, or even threatening became illuminated when examined in the light of a more familiar practice or custom. Also the practices of one's familiar religion would take on new significance when found to have certain aspects universal to the human religious impulse.

Campbell said, "When I started teaching comparative mythology, I was afraid I might destroy my student's religious beliefs, but what I found was just the opposite. Religious traditions, which didn't mean very much to my students, but which were the ones their parents had given them, suddenly became illumined in a new way when we compared them with other traditions, where similar images had been given a more inward or spiritual interpretation."

Campbell continued, "I had Christian students, Jewish students, Buddhist students, a couple of Zoroastrian students—they all had this experience. There's no danger in interpreting the symbols of a religious system and calling them metaphors instead of facts. What that does is to turn them into messages for your own inward experience and life. The system suddenly becomes a personal experience."[PPP]

Campbell's insight about interpreting the symbols and stories of a religious tradition as metaphors instead of facts was the critical piece for me. This opened up whole new vistas of understanding of the Hebrew and Greek scriptures that make up the Bible. Once I was exposed to parallels of these stories in other religious traditions, I realized these stories originate from deep within the human psyche, and this gave them universal psychological significance. Creation stories, flood stories, virgin births, and deifications of heroes—these motifs have arisen spontaneously in many cultures all around the world.

It is only as people venture out and receive messages from distant lands and different people that they gain the perspective necessary to uncover the treasure that exists in their own homes and hearts. Sometimes it's only as we leave home that we can come home and truly know home. This is the paradox of the story that makes it a lesson for the ages. It's something people can never fully grasp with analytical minds. Outsiders often see certain things more clearly, and encounters with them can function as mirrors to see things in new, insightful ways.

A few years ago, I got to know an Indian woman named Nemarla. Her husband was a medical colleague of mine. They had immigrated to the United States many years before. Once during a brief encounter, I expressed some curiosity about her culture, and she offered to give me a book explaining Hindu religion and ways of life. I stopped by her husband's office a few days later to pick up the book. Nemarla was there and seemed anxious that we continue our conversation. She seemed to sense an attentive presence in me and was delighted to discover someone who genuinely wanted to learn more about her faith. They had been living in this small community for twenty years, yet they still felt excluded because of their religion. Despite being successful economically, they had felt much loneliness and frustration in their private lives since moving to this country.

Friendships had been hard for them to come by. People in our small town were friendly enough, but after exchanging pleasantries, acquaintances usually wanted to shift the conversation around to religion. When the conversation veered in this direction, people only wanted to tell her how great their churches were. If she explained she was Hindu, they usually let the matter drop. However, Nemarla was respectful of them and listened attentively, and so many times they would ask her if she had accepted Jesus. She would say, "I know Jesus. He is a great man and a great teacher."

Then they would press her further. "Have you accepted him as your personal savior?" Sometimes they would even tell her the consequences if she had not.

Nemarla became visibly agitated at this point in our conversation. I will never forget the words she used as she finished this story. She said, "I think people that act like this are an insult to Jesus." The irony of that moment was not lost on me. It took someone from a completely different religion than Christianity to convey an aspect of the character of Jesus that rang true. Those words lodged in my brain, and I pondered them for many days.

It is popular to say in the Christian community that Jesus is love. There is a big difference, though, between hearing about a loving person and being loved by a person. That is the critical issue that simply doesn't get through to most people who claim to know Jesus. In encounters with people of other faiths, the Christian community seems well intentioned in its efforts to tell others about Jesus, but they forget to act like Jesus toward them. Jesus almost always approached others with a listening ear. He almost always began conversations with a question. For him love was always an active demonstration of interest in their personhoods and not a conversion effort.

Openness to the people and ideas of different religions seems consistent with the character of Jesus as he is revealed in the Gospel stories. In the few instances where he encountered those from a different culture, he held them in high regard. He even held them up as examples of great faith, as he did with the Roman centurion.[23] Converting them to his way of thinking did not seem to be a part of Jesus's agenda. He often invited them to go deeper in thinking and processing matters of faith, as he did with the Samaritan woman. He suggested to her that where people worshipped was not so important; it was rather the spirit in which someone approached God that mattered.[24] It would seem that his end goal was not to dissuade the woman from her religious tradition but to invite her to explore it more deeply.

At its heart that seems to be the message of Rabbi Eisik's story also. He took courage in hand and made the journey to a far-off place. He listened intently to the message of another. However, he recognized he had to do his own reflection and work. He persevered and did so. He went back to his home to do the real digging. Following the metaphor of the story, he dug deeper into his own tradition and faith in order to find the real riches buried there. Going back to home and trusting it contains a store of riches is just as much a part of the story's message as is setting out to follow some far-off dream in the first place.

---

23 Luke 7:1–10.

24 John 4:7–30.

Another story might serve to illustrate. A wise teacher once said that when people need water, it is better to dig a single one hundred-foot well than to dig ten ten-foot wells. Those who fail to dig beneath the obstructing rocks and continually quit and move on in search of easier ground will never reach water. It is possible to find water of spiritual refreshment in all faiths, but one must be willing to do the hard work even when the digging gets difficult.

* * *

twenty four

Healing the Wounds of
Our Religious Past

The Navigators is an evangelical Christian organization that targets people in the armed forces. Think of it as Campus Crusade for Christ geared more toward military bases than college campuses. When I was in college, the Navigators had an extremely active group at the nearby Moody Air Force Base. This was primarily due to the talents of their leader, a man named Ric. Ric was such a dynamic and engaging speaker that his influence spread well beyond the air force base. By the time I entered Valdosta State College as a freshman in 1972, he was attracting many students from the campus to go hear him preach every Sunday evening at a location near the campus.

Not long after my arrival at Valdosta State, I got an opportunity to hear this preacher who many of my friends were talking about. To this day I'm not sure if it was because I was young and impressionable, whether I got caught up in the madness of the crowd, or whether Ric was really that much of a charismatic personality, but he soon enthralled me as well. Never did I miss a chance to hear Ric speak or be involved in whatever he was promoting.

Around spring semester there was to be this big Navigator convention in Pensacola, and Ric was planning to take along a busload of people from Valdosta. Naturally I wanted to go along. Ric's followers were having a car wash at a nearby shopping center to raise money for our transportation costs. I was in the middle of this effort.

It was one of those swelteringly hot summer days in Valdosta. The water running off those washed cars was causing steam to rise from the asphalt. We had gotten permission to wash the cars behind the buildings at this shopping center, and so our operation was not visible from the main road. I got assigned to take the first shift doing the really hot job of going out in the street, holding up the sign, and shouting at the people with dirty cars. Like a good disciple, I did what I was told. Confident someone would come relieve me at some point so that I would at least get a chance to get wet and get something to drink, I stayed at my post. Around two o'clock that afternoon, I had been out there about four hours, and no one else ever showed up to spell me.

Hot, tired, and hungry, I finally gave up my post and walked back around the buildings on the other side of the shopping center. The car wash was over, and everyone had left except Ric. He was packing up some hoses and was about to leave himself. I approached him and complained that no one had ever come to relieve me so I could go get some lunch. As he climbed in his car, his only response was, "Well, if only you and God knew about that, then that would be a good deal." And he drove off. That was one of his pet phrases he used in his preaching—good deal. Everything that was Godly was as good deal. Going on this trip to Pensacola was supposed to be a good deal. Now Ric was telling me it would have been a good deal if I had not complained but had chosen to suffer silently.

I got such a flash of insight then. In an instant I realized Ric and everything he stood for was a crock. Thankfully I was well enough grounded in my own sense of self-worth to recognize his words as an attempt to lay undeserved guilt upon me. I was also given the grace to begin to see him as a total fraud. In retrospect my only regret is that I didn't have the courage to say to him, "You self-righteous b*******."

I did learn a lot from this incident, however, about the potential for a powerful, revered religious leader to oppress, manipulate, and control his or her followers through shame and guilt.

I acknowledge this incident is rather trivial compared to episodes of religious abuse others have suffered. All too often the newspapers contain stories of pastors extorting money and sex from their parishioners, a young woman trying to commit suicide after her minister tells her she is so stained with sin there is no hope for her, or a young man putting a shotgun in his mouth and pulling the trigger because his family and church convince him he is no good because of his homosexual tendencies. The list goes on.

What is religious or spiritual abuse? (I use the terms "religious abuse" and "spiritual abuse" interchangeably.) Like any form of abuse, it occurs when a person or group with power uses that power to hurt. In the case of religious abuse, the wounds are not visible. However, the damage can be much more severe because it goes to the spirit and psyche—the very core of people. Because the wounds are hidden and the damage is insidious, ferreting out the perpetrators can be difficult. Further complicating the issue is the very nature of religion and spirituality. Religious abusers can be curiously naïve about the effects of their abusive behavior because they are so focused on some nebulous goals they are trying to accomplish for God. They can easily lose sight of the narcissism that motivates their actions. So they move through society gaining great status and great groups of followers but leaving behind an invisible trail of spiritual wounds and corpses.

Who are the victims? Anyone who is lonely, emotionally immature, or lacking in the ability to differentiate in healthy ways from the power of groupthink is susceptible to becoming a victim of religious abuse. It's not hard to see there's a tremendous percentage of the population at risk. Given the relative lack of spiritual development, emotional maturity, and ability to think critically out there, it's really a sign of grace that religious abuse is not much more prevalent than it already is.

How does it happen? The basic mechanism religious abusers use is coercion, exploitation, or control. The perpetrators capitalize on the victims' distorted views of God as harsh and judgmental. This couples with the victims' vulnerability in taking on guilt and shame. The perpetrators are skillful in the use of the religious language of the community to assume positions of authority and to manipulate susceptible victims into positions of submission and subordination. It's really not that difficult to accomplish given the general perception in most cultures that religious institutions and religious leaders are the very foundation of the community's morality and ethics. These leaders and institutions suck people in. After all, isn't going to church supposed to be the "right" thing to do? By blindly putting faith in the goodness of anything associated with the church, synagogue, temple, or ashram, the groundwork is laid for all sorts of unhealthy behaviors to take place and dysfunctional systems to develop.

We're spiritually progressive, though. Right? We're open to differing religious views, able to think critically, and use our capacity for spiritual discernment wisely. What does religious abuse have to do with us?

Given how widespread religious abuse is, there likely are some who have suffered religious abuse in the past in virtually every community. Unless the abused person has gotten counseling or managed to gain healing insight on their own (unlikely), the wounds remain. The problem persists. To understand this requires the grasp of a fundamental psychological principle known as reaction formation.

Whenever people react strongly to or reject a value or belief system, there is a human tendency to turn 180 degrees. For example, if the concept of a harsh and angry God has hurt someone, and their defense mechanisms are sufficiently strong to lead them out of that draconian environment, they often declare themselves atheists or agnostics. The term "a-theist" indicates they are self-defining in relationship to what they are against—theism. (Nontheist is a more descriptive term for the person who is sincere and not merely reactive.) They are not describing the positive values of what they are for or what new identity they are growing into. Herein lies the danger. If several members of a group have similar experiences of hurt, and they go to the opposite extreme by reacting strongly against that which wounded, then they never heal. They are just as dependent on the person or religious institution that hurt them as they ever were because its existence is necessary for their self-definitions. Constant reactivity in the face of anything that reminds such individuals of what hurt them keeps the wounds festering and prevents them from gaining any nourishment from the deeper truths of that religion or mythology. It also prevents them from being able to offer healing to others who might be trying to escape abusive situations of their own. So much of their energy goes into nursing their own wounds that they have nothing nourishing and positive to offer others.

To look at this another way, we can simply say that religion affects us all. Declaring yourself in utter rejection to a belief system is to be just as controlled by it as someone who is an active participant. The pervasive nature of religion in the world creates an inescapable environs. It is as much a part of life on this planet as air. To say religion does not affect you at all is to suggest you are in complete denial of your real nature and the nature of life on this planet.

To be spiritually healthy, all people must come to grips with the true nature of what has hurt them. It is not a religion or a belief system that hurts. It is a dysfunctional person or group of people within that religion. If reminders of previous people or religious institutions still affect the victims so strongly that they can't be in relationships with others who still cling to that institution, then they are still surrendering to the authority of that person or institution. It still holds them in its grasp, whether they will admit it or not.

Healing requires time and effort. Having a safe place to tell the story without fear of retribution or being ostracized is a necessary part of that healing. That's why support groups work. However, telling the story to someone who has been hurt in similar ways (someone who only supports and validates the anger and reactivity without facilitating our healing and growth beyond them) is not necessarily healing. Often that validation perpetuates denial. Being affirmed in these smoldering negative emotions might feel good for a moment but leaves the underlying wound as dangerous as ever.

The world desperately needs more individuals and more communities that can provide healing to the spiritually wounded. To become a such a healing presence requires us to examine our own wounds and be healed of them. Only then can we show others the way to be healed and how to be whatever they are called to be rather than just reacting to the toxicity of literal, fundamental religion. As we discover how to be in community in healthy ways, we then can become not only a healing balm for spiritual abuse but also an inoculation against it. If we are willing to do the real work on ourselves and our community that this requires, then we will have so much more to offer a hurting world.

* * *

twenty five

What Kind of People Shall We Be?

I recall the time when my son, Dustin, was in high school, and his class was exploring cultures from different parts of the world. As a part of their studies, each student was to put together a visual display of the particular culture they had selected so that all the students could see the exhibits in the school hallway during World Culture Day. The exhibits were to contain, among other things, numerous art objects indicative of the culture. When the exhibits appeared, some parents protested loudly when the child who had chosen India included a representation of a dancing Shiva as part of the exhibit. The teacher calmly attempted to explain it is difficult to separate religious iconography from art when representing Eastern cultures, but the parents persisted in their protests. They cited the Establishment Clause of the constitution and laws against the use of religious symbols in public places. Incensed that their children could not partake in a Christian prayer in school, they were not about to let any suggestion of devotion from another religion enter into the school system. The dancing Shiva and all the colorful artwork with Hindu symbology were removed from the exhibit. Sterilized in such a way, the exhibit met all the legal requirements for a display in a public place. Whether it now gave the observer a true visual immersion in the richness of the oldest continuous civilization in the world was more questionable.

The United States champions freedom of religion in the private sphere. However, when religion encroaches on public and political life, it seems the only way to maintain freedom of religion is to keep it free from religion. Religious tolerance scarcely has a chance to emerge as a virtue because the public discourse largely skirts all mention of religious faith. By keeping religion out of public life, tolerance has dissolved into indifference.

However, the public square can't simply be sterilized from something as basic to human beings as the religious or spiritual impulse. If people are mindful enough to be on the lookout for it, they'll notice that religion has not disappeared from the public arena. It's still there, and when it makes one of its rare public appearances, it often offers a chance to see the fundamentalist mind-set at work. I'd like to take you behind the scenes of one of these occasions.

Nothing seems to test the civility of a community more than when religion appears in public. In my local community, it does every year the first week of May with two National Days of Prayer in Lowndes County, Georgia.

These two events differ in important ways. At the first one (the one I choose not to participate in) only Christians are welcome to speak, and only Christians who agree with a particular evangelical view of Christianity are able to volunteer as coordinators. In many if not most cities across the country where organized National Day of Prayer observances take place, these guidelines are followed because the National Day of Prayer Task Force demands it. For an inclusive ceremony to occur, local religious leaders must take it upon themselves to organize one. That happened here in Lowndes County through the initiative of my congregation members and others who felt that more diverse voices should be added to the collective prayers.

Many questions arise around the National Day of Prayer phenomenon and what response, if any, it demands. I do not profess to have all the answers. These questions are merely part of a couple extremely important larger questions.

1) What should the relationship as Christians be with other faith traditions?
2) How should people respond when the only voices being heard publicly are exclusive of the religious views of other faith traditions?

As I attempted to answer these questions, my thoughts took the shape of another question. What kind of people shall we be in a world where some claim our Christian identity yet practice exclusive religion? I came up with many different answers. Each revealed a certain dimension of the problem in fundamentalist thinking. These answers are incomplete and not entirely satisfactory, but they might begin a conversation and get people to think more deeply about what everyone loses in terms of identity when the fundamentalists are the only voices being heard in the public arena.

Shall we be a quiet people? Many people merely shrug at the idea of a National Day of Prayer. Perhaps they see (quite rightly) that many of the principals involved in this grandstand piety are after good press more than any heartfelt need to express corporate concern for the sufferings of humanity. For many prayer is a private matter, and praying for others is OK as a way to show care and concern. In public prayer, though, the speaker ends up speaking for other people and imposing a specific theology. Prayers addressed to a God who would open the rain clouds on some and not on others, choose to heal someone who previously he had chosen to neglect, and always run out onto the field with one team, church, and nation, this is not my understanding of God. Prayer is a much-maligned concept. Janis Joplin even playfully satirized it in her 1971 hit "Mercedes Benz" where she asks the Lord to buy her the car. No wonder many want no part of a ceremony reminiscent of other occasions where this kind of deity was invoked.

Nonparticipation is a choice, and in some circumstances it seems to be the right one for many. One people can make with honesty and integrity. As I said I will not be participating in the noon ceremony on the first Thursday in May, not that that would be an option for me. I would likely be refused a voice. However, rather than be quiet in the face of this, I was excited when I was approached about the possibility of organizing an inclusive Prayer Day ceremony. I firmly believe there is a void of religious leadership in the world, and if the conservative, evangelical community is the only one speaking publically, people will listen to them because they feel there is nowhere else to turn. People need to hear the voices of the more open-minded, so I am there to add to the multicultural chorus. Mine is a faith tradition that actively seeks to move beyond mere tolerance to inclusivity and even pluralism. Each person can gain a slightly better perspective on the divine in and through the public sharing of innermost yearnings.

Shall we be an angry people? In October 2008 the Freedom from Religion Foundation filed a lawsuit against President Bush and the National Day of Prayer Task Force. It charged that the National Day of Prayer was unconstitutional and created a hostile environment. Other groups such as Jews on First and the Interfaith Alliance were understandably upset about the billing of the website of the Task Force as the "official" website of the National Day of Prayer. Giving the Task Force further credibility in branding itself as an official government entity, President Bush celebrated NDP for eight years with prominent evangelicals in the East Room of the White House. Feelings were running high among many groups on both sides of this issue of inclusivity versus exclusivity.

Sometimes there is a place for righteous anger. Sometimes it yields beneficial action. One response to the NDP phenomenon was the establishment of a National Day of Reason in 2003 to coincide with the NDP on the first Thursday in May. Various humanist, agnostic, and atheist groups started this celebration to show how to bring about beneficial social change in alternative ways to prayer. One way they do this is to organize blood drives during their events.

Shall we be a courageous people? Fundamentalism is based in fear—fear of modernity, change, loss of control, strangers, and the "other." It takes courage to attempt to respond to it, but everyone must. Providing an alternate model of community, as the inclusive prayer service does, is one constructive response. Building and maintaining personal connections is another. Coming to some understanding of how the fundamentalist mind works is also helpful.

Since fundamentalism is grounded in fear, institutions and ways of thinking that provide rigid structure lessen that fear. This provides great comfort to fundamentalist followers, and that is why they cling to the trappings and the dogma of religion so vehemently. Issues are processed as black and white. Relying on strict codes of good and evil, fundamentalists want clear-cut answers to the complexities of life. Thinking in terms of both/and rather than either/or seems to be a real stretch for the fundamentalist.

Fundamentalist Christians, for example, are likely to tell people that either they believe in Jesus Christ or they are going to hell. Either they are Christians or they are not. Clear-cut. Plain and simple. A fixed perception. Hence either/or thinking dominates their religious ideology and is the basis for how they form exclusive views of what it takes to be saved, to be a Christian, or to be accepted into the religious community.

Then a both/and thinker comes along and frames things in a way that seems beyond the ability of an either/or thinker to comprehend. Take perhaps the greatest example of both/and thinking—Gandhi's statement when asked about his religion. "I am a Muslim, and a Hindu, and a Christian, and a Jew." Multidimensional. Paradoxical. Such complex thinking alludes to the oneness beneath the universe and the uniting of all humanity in a common quest to grasp great mystery. Jesus was into paradoxical, both/and thinking as well. "The last will be first and the first will be last."[25] "Those who find their life will lose it, and those who lose their life for my sake will find it."[26] Fundamentalist Christians, while adamant about some things Jesus said, don't seem to invoke these sayings very much.

Shall we be a loving people? I would like to say that all progressive Christians are able to think in multidimensional, paradoxical terms, but we have our own either/or thinkers as well. It seems beyond the comprehension of some progressives that one can be a Christian and a practicing Buddhist as well. There is such a wide spectrum of theological perspectives in Christian churches. Yes, there are still many out there who read in the Bible that Christ is coming and think he is going to literally float in on a cloud and set up his kingdom on Earth. However, there is a significant number of Christians who read that Christ is coming and hear that as meaning that the Christ nature, which is potentially there in every human heart, is being increasingly awakened as humanity develops and is slowly but surely fulfilling its full potential to embrace truth and love. These are the kindred spirits Francis David, the founder of the Unitarian faith in Transylvania, probably had in mind when he said, "We need not think alike to love alike."

The vast majority of ministers in the local ministerial association are professing Christians, and I'm delighted that they regularly participate in our inclusive Prayer Day service. I'm proud of this group and the stand they take to build community. They say by their

---

25 Matt. 20:16.
26 Matt. 10:39.

actions what we say in one responsive reading. "If you are Hindu, and I am Christian, it will not matter." This is just one example of how by growing up spiritually we can create a more peaceful, loving world.

* * *

twenty six

Resurrecting the Resurrection

Several Easters ago a man named David Storch was returning a book he had borrowed from the Brooklyn Public Library. The book was a beautifully bound score of Handel's *Messiah*. David was a music professor and choral conductor at a local community college. He had borrowed the book for his school's annual Easter performance of the beloved choral piece.

What David didn't know as he made his way to the library with book in hand was that due to a glitch in the library's computer system, the book he had checked out a couple weeks before had not been marked as checked out. There was no record of where the book was or who had it. It appeared in the library's online database as available.

The *Messiah* is a very popular piece during Easter, so many others conductors, when they learned through the library's online database that it was available, came to check it out.

When they arrived, however, they were all disappointed. The book was nowhere to be found. This led to a frantic search, and for three days the anxious library staff looked everywhere for the book. They hoped it had just been misplaced or misfiled. After exhausting all possibilities, they finally gave up and marked the book as missing.

When Storch walked into the library with the score to Handel's *Messiah*, a young librarian was working the circulation desk along with a dozen or so people sitting quietly at tables. When he put the book down on the desk, the young librarian took one look at it, forgot where she was for a moment, and shouted with sheer delight. "It's the *Messiah*! The *Messiah* is here!"

A surge of energy went through the library. Everyone looked up astonished, but when they saw it was just a librarian holding a book, they all put their heads down and went back to work.

The librarian's words are faintly reminiscent of the scene from that very first Easter morning recorded in the Gospel of John. This details how early in the morning Mary Magdalene went alone to the tomb where Jesus was buried. Finding the stone rolled away and the body gone, she began to weep. A man appeared to her who she supposed was the gardener, and she asked him, "Sir, if you have carried him away, tell me where you have laid him, and I will take him away." When the man said her name, she immediately recognized this man to be Jesus. Overcome with excitement, she ran to the other disciples and announced to them, "I have seen the Lord!"[27]

The traditional story of Easter goes something like this. Jesus was crucified on Good Friday and buried in a tomb that was sealed with a rock. Somehow the rock got rolled away, and three days later he was miraculously resurrected. He appeared in bodily form to several of his followers after his resurrection before ascending to heaven. Because of his divine status and his appointment to be a sacrifice for sin, people gain forgiveness and eternal life when they believe this story about him and accept him as their savior.

27 John 20:1–18.

I would submit that the story is about so much more than whether one man survived bodily death some two thousand years ago—an idea that seems rather absurd to the rational twenty-first-century mind. To really get at what the resurrection story is about, some critical questions are necessary. What might have prompted the authors of the Gospels to compose such an incredible story? What can be said for sure about that period in Jewish history? These are the types of questions asked in the academic community in the process of doing credible, reliable, critical biblical scholarship.

Here's a brief summary of current scholastic thinking on the matter. First, the idea of resurrection was well known to the first-century Jews. It's present in the Old Testament, in passages such as Ezekiel's metaphorical vision of new life for the skeletons in the valley of the dry bones. It can also be heard in Isaiah's lyrical prophesy that though the virtuous now suffer and die someday they will overcome. In Isaiah's own words, "your dead shall live, and their corpses shall rise."[28] Second, the followers of Jesus endured tremendous persecution in the wake of his death. The powers that be who crucified Jesus did not suddenly disappear after he was gone. His followers lived under the same threat as Jesus did, and they had the vivid reminder of what the ruling elites had done to their leader. Jesus's followers would not have wanted the Roman legions and the Jewish Sanhedrin to have the last word. This is the backdrop out of which the story of Jesus's resurrection came forth. As the theologian Harvey Cox says, resurrection stories did "not have to do with immortality. They are about God's justice. They are an expression of a human hope that is born of a moral, not a metaphysical, impulse. They did not spring up from a yearning for life after death, but from the conviction that ultimately a truly just God simply has to vindicate the victims of the callous and the powerful."[QQQ]

---

28   Isaiah 26:19.

The stories that the Gospel writers told came out of this kind of understanding of resurrection. When Mark said, "Why do you seek the living among the dead," he wasn't referring to some sort of magical, metaphysical sleight of hand where Jesus disappeared here and reappeared over there. He was telling a story that spoke to his people about hope in the midst of their own oppressive circumstances. He was saying the Roman legions would not have the final say. When Luke recorded Jesus's followers seeing him after the crucifixion and when the ate together on the road to Emmaus, he was saying (as profoundly and poetically as he could in the only language he had available to him) that one would only see Jesus when one went to the same places he went and inhabited the same circles he inhabited.

It's very easy to shoot holes in the biblical story of the resurrection from a post-Enlightenment, postscientific, twenty-first-century perspective. The story wasn't written as history, and to interpret it as such distorts its original meaning. When the story is read as history today, it leads to some bizzare and rather amusing speculations. For example, every now and then someone in the Holy Land will unearth an ossuary containing bony fragments and bearing the name of Jesus (a rather common Jewish name in ancient Palestine). When this happens, the world is forced to endure another round of scientific theories about what might have happened to the molecules that composed Jesus's body.

However, reading the Gospel stories as poetic prose—the way they are meant to be read—it satisfies even the most critical biblical scholars. It gives a logical and credible way to understand the resurrection accounts in the Gospels. However, it also raises an even more important question. If that was the what and why of the story of Jesus's resurrection and how it came into being in the first century, how are people to understand that story today? What possible theological significance could it have in today's world?

For an answer to that question, I turn to the postmodern Christian theologian Peter Rollins, who grew up in Northern Ireland during the time of its most intense violence. He developed his theology amid the ruins caused by the religious strife there. Rollins never fails to get the best of the Christian establishment when they try to pin him down on his theological views. Quoting a statement he made in one of his books, a reporter recently asked him if he denied the resurrection of Christ. His answer:

> "I can without equivocation or hesitation fully and completely admit that I deny the resurrection of Christ. This is something that anyone who knows me could tell you, and I am not afraid to say it publicly, no matter what some people may think...
>
> I deny the resurrection of Christ every time I do not serve at the feet of the oppressed, each day that I turn my back on the poor; I deny the resurrection of Christ when I close my ears to the cries of the downtrodden and lend my support to an unjust and corrupt system.
>
> However there are moments when I affirm that resurrection, few and far between as they are. I affirm it when I stand up for those who are forced to live on their knees, when I speak for those who have had their tongues torn out, when I cry for those who have no more tears left to shed."RRR

Resurrection is not merely about one human mysteriously overcoming death some two thousand years ago. That story is indeed a powerful one and has captured the human imagination in ways no other story has before or since. However, resurrections happen every day if there is poet enough within our hearts and minds to recognize them and call them forth.

My own wife, Kathy, is dealing with lung cancer right now. In order to cope with the potential outcome of this very serious, life-threatening illness, we have had to find a way to move forward and get through each day. It's nice to say we want to live each moment to the fullest, and we very much try to do just that. As a mantra, we use the idea of living every day as if it's the last one we will ever have together. This is a good thought to return to every time the disease itself, the tests, or the treatments throws us another curve. However, life still puts before us the same ordinary problems and frustrations it presents to everyone else. Even with a serious disease, bills still have to be paid, taxes still have to be done, other drivers still cut us off when we're trying to change lanes, and the family still squabbles.

Something that has been helpful for us going forward is to draw a distinction between hope and optimism. Optimism is maintaining an expectant attitude of a particular outcome. In our case optimism would mean looking for the best of all possibilities. Optimism would be Kathy's scans showing the cancer no longer active, or that she will be cured of the cancer. While these thoughts do exist somewhere in our thought processes, to put too much focus on them is highly problematic and sets us up for disappointment. If we were to continually dwell in optimism, and we got a less-than-optimal result from her tests or treatments, then we would feel disappointed, bitter, or even betrayed.

Hope, on the other hand, is less specific but more open, enduring, and creative. Hope is an expectant attitude that looks for possibility in whatever life presents to us. Hope always keeps possibilities before us that something good or useful can come out of any circumstances no matter what. There is always something to hope for—more time with family, a chance to encourage someone else with this disease, the possibility of focusing on what's really important, or saying and doing those things we've always put off. When we're hopeful, we still look the realities of the situation squarely in the face but always manage to find meaning and creative purpose within it all.

The Easter story is just that—a story. It was likely meant to bring hope to a community caught in a seemingly hopeless situation. Easter, however, isn't something that might or might not have happened two millennia ago. Easter happens every day when people act in the world as agents of hope. When people live their lives in this way, they bear witness to Easter. When they act in ways that put hope and possibility before another human being, they're plotting a resurrection. Maybe it's the possibility of a full stomach, a better tomorrow, or that one day the moral arc of the universe will bend toward justice. Perhaps it's the possibility that something good can come from what today appears hopeless.

To bring hope is to bring life—new life where once there was none. Bringing hope requires we remain faithful to our commitments and that we enter into community with each other with a sense of expectancy, knowing that sometimes it's going to require us to be creative and flexible. Resurrection is not merely about one human overcoming death. Resurrection is more about all humanity overcoming darkness and despair to emerge from these things that entomb the soul into the light of hope and courage and purpose.

* * *

twenty seven

Why I Still Self-Identify as a Christian

*"I am a Muslim. And a Hindu. And a Christian.
And a Jew. And so are all of you."*
—Mohandas Gandhi, *admonishing his separatist followers*

The following is a familiar Zen Buddhist story.

Two monks were returning to their monastery after a long day working in the fields. As they walked, the eager young monk asked the elder monk many questions about the dharma and about life.

It had rained heavily that day, and as they approached a stream they had crossed easily that morning, they noticed it had swollen to many times its earlier size, and the current was now quite strong. They also noticed a lovely young woman sitting by the bank of the river looking very distressed. The elder monk asked her if they could be of any assistance. She said she must get to the other side but was afraid to cross. While the young monk hesitated, the elder monk quickly picked the young woman up in his arms and carried her over to the other side. The younger monk said nothing

204

but followed behind them. When they reached the other bank, the woman thanked the monk and went on her way. The monks resumed their trip to the monastery in silence. It was obvious the younger monk was brooding and preoccupied. When they reached the gate of the monastery, the young monk confronted the elder one. "We have been taught not to even look at women and certainly not to touch them. And here you have picked one up and carried her!"

The elder monk opened the gate and calmly replied, "I put that young woman down many miles back. How is it that you are carrying her still?"[SSS]

Have you have ever felt guilty for something you've done? It's not a very good feeling, is it? You do something wrong, intentionally or not, and you end up hurting someone else. Guilt is a pretty universal human phenomenon. Many times when we feel guilt, we carry it around for hours, days, or sometimes, in a more grievous offense where someone suffered permanent emotional or physical harm, a lifetime. Guilt can be some pretty hefty baggage to carry around for an entire life's journey.

Guilt, though, is not necessarily a bad thing. If people are living their lives in ways that repeatedly harm others, it's a good thing for them to feel bad about it. If they feel badly about what they're doing and experience guilt, they're much more likely to make some sort of correction in their thinking or habitual ways of doing things and this can prevent them from causing injury or suffering in the future. As the psychiatrist Willard Gaylin says, "Guilt is the guardian of our goodness."[TTT] We need a certain amount of guilt to exist well. This "existential guilt" serves as a sort of self-corrective mechanism.

People who lack this self-corrective mechanism are some of the most toxic, dangerous people on the face of the Earth. Psychologists have a special name for them. They're called sociopaths. People with impaired capacities to feel guilt are unlikely to develop behaviors that reflect a basic concern for others. Without guilt they have no internal moral compasses, and they can cause no end of pain and heartache for those around them. Often sociopaths end up in prison, but they are just as likely to appear successful. They can be clever at disguising their lack of a conscience and are quite determined to get what they want. Unfortunately on their way to what appears outwardly to be success, they leave broad swaths of pain and destruction.

So guilt or remorse can function in our lives to shape us into better people. However, it's a heavy burden. Guilt can wreak all sorts of havoc if carried around unnecessarily.

That's just one of many good takeaways that we might get from the story of the two monks. The elder monk is unconcerned that he broke a social taboo. He's unconcerned about the letter of the law for his community. His focus is on the spirit of the law, and that is to be compassionate and serve others. The young monk is too intent on doing what's right as opposed to doing what's good and compassionate. He's obviously too focused on what others might think about a monk who dared touch a woman. The elder monk is wise enough to not only do the compassionate thing but to do it without hesitation or guilt.

The teaching of the story is useful—up to a point. Touching a woman and carrying her across the creek is, after all, pretty lightweight stuff. The worst that could have happened would be the tarnishing of the monk's image or that of his community in the eyes of the townspeople had they seen or heard about the incident. Likely no one would have been physically or psychologically damaged.

In real life the burden of guilt can be and often is much greater. Life's messy, and we often hurt others. Sometimes we do so unintentionally. Sometimes it's a direct effect of dysfunctional behavior. When others suffer because of something we have done or failed to do, we hurt also. What are we supposed to do with that hurt and that burden of guilt? I don't think there's a Zen story or a meditation technique that can take that burden away.

Have you ever heard of the book *I'm OK, You're OK*? OK, I'm showing my age here. The book was immensely popular during the self-help craze of the sixties and seventies. Like any popular work, its title got parodied many times. George Carlin had an entire comedy routine that dissed the whole self-help craze. The routine was called, "I Suck, You Suck." Perhaps, though, the most insightful parody of the title (one that imparts an important kernel of wisdom even as it amuses) was the saying that developed in Alcoholics Anonymous and other twelve-step groups. "I'm not OK, and you're not OK. But that's OK."

AA and other twelve-step groups are so successful largely because they offer ways to proactively approach the burden of guilt that so many carry. Guilt is difficult to escape, and that's partly why so many people turn to drugs, alcohol, and other escapist routes. The twelve steps give addicts an alternative, more constructive path to deal with the pain guilt brings. Group members are asked to humble themselves and admit they are powerless to deal with their problems (to admit they're not OK), to turn it over to God or some other higher power, to take a searching and fearless moral inventory of themselves, and to attempt when possible to make amends to those whom their actions have harmed. Those who are ready and willing to submit themselves to the discipline of the twelve steps find there is power in powerlessness. Their guilt can be expiated or overcome as they surrender themselves to a power greater than themselves. They can enjoy the support of others who have borne the same burden. We don't have to be alcoholics or drug addicts to realize there are shortcomings in our lives, and we could also benefit from the discipline the twelve steps offer.

Sometimes people find it rather curious that I'm a Unitarian Universalist minister, but I also self-identify as a Christian. After all, I'm often critical of Christianity in my sermons for its rather unimaginative ways of portraying the afterlife, for its exclusive portrayal of Jesus as the one and only incarnation, and for how this way of understanding Jesus alienates people of other faith traditions. I often quarrel with Christianity, but it's a lover's quarrel. I do love and embrace Christianity, but I do so *only* when discussing the Gospel message as I've come to understand it from my reading and studying of the New Testament. I'm not talking about Christianity as it's generally taught in most Christian churches today. Often that teaching only seems to amount to a way to divide the world into the "saved" and the "unsaved."

There are several reasons I embrace Christianity. I'm only going to give the main reason, though. Of all the world's religions, Christianity has the best answer to the problem of guilt.

To talk about this, I'm going to have to use a word that most, myself included, don't like—sin. It's a word loaded with preconceptions built up over centuries as the institutional church has used it to convict people and keep them under its power. The word conjures up images of hellfire and damnation sermons, of little old ladies preoccupied with sex and how to morally condemn the younger generation, and even of Eve handing Adam an apple. This act has come to be known as the "original sin," even though that term is never used in the story or even in the Bible.

The word "sin" simply means "missing the mark." It's a word from archery. To say one sins means one often misses the mark or can't hit the bull's eye every time. Sometimes we do the wrong thing, and sometimes we fail to do the right thing. We aren't perfect. We're all sinners. We cannot not sin.

That's one side of the paradox. The other side is that no matter what we've done, what sin we've committed, or how guilty we feel, there is forgiveness available. If we confess our sins and experience genuine contrition or remorse for what we've done, then we can be forgiven. In Christian parlance, God forgives us. We cannot not sin, but fortunately God is unfailingly forgiving. This isn't an abdication of responsibility for what we've done. Far from that. It means we're willing to accept full responsibility for our actions, and we're willing to demonstrate the sincerity of our contrition by making restitution whenever possible. Existentially, though, it is as if the slate is wiped clean. It's as if the sin never happened.

There's a lovely story to illustrate this. There was once a little Filipino girl who claimed she talked to Jesus. Initially people laughed and thought this was sweet, but the more the little girl talked about it, the more convinced the people became there really was something extraordinary going on. Word got around to the bishop about this little girl and her visions of talking to Jesus. He decided he needed to check this out. So he sent for the little girl and had her brought to the cathedral. After spending quite a bit of time with her, the bishop was convinced of her innocence and sincerity but really didn't know whether to put any credence in the validity of her claim. He decided, therefore, to put her to a test. The bishop had been rather rowdy as a youth and had gotten into no end of trouble during his days in the seminary. He remembered that he had recently confessed one of these sins. He said to the little girl, "When you talk to Jesus again, would you ask him what it was that I confessed to the last time I went to the confessional?"

The little girl said she would. The next day the bishop, barely able to conceal his eagerness, asked her, "Have you talked to Jesus since we last met?" She said she had. So he asked her, "Well, when you asked him what I had confessed to, what did he say?"

Her reply was, "He said, 'I've forgotten.'"[UUU]

Even based on this evidence, the bishop could not say for sure one way or another whether this little girl really had talked to Jesus. Her theology, though, was very sound. Once we confess our sins with contrition, it's as if they no longer exist. This is how, in

Christian understanding, guilt is expiated, sin is forgiven, and we find atonement ("at-one-ment") with God again.

Not only does Christianity have this doctrine of atonement, but it also has a ritual that enacts the same spiritual dynamic. It's called communion. Ideally church members are not to take communion unless they have confessed their sins. By taking in the wine and wafer, which represent the body and blood of Jesus, we are recognizing our dependence on the forgiveness of God, manifested in Jesus, for our sins. By acknowledging this and enacting this ritual with others within the Church community, we are relieved of our burdens of guilt and once again made whole.

As the Unitarian faith reclaims its religious roots in Christianity, it can appropriate the healing balm of this doctrine of atonement. When the Unitarians rejected the theological ideas of original sin and the inherent depravity of humanity, it also moved away from the psychological and spiritual reality that as humans we are flawed, and we often bear tremendous burdens of guilt. Unitarian theology rightly rejected the idea humans are miserable sinners in the hands of an angry God who holds us over the fiery flames of hell. In the process, though, it seems to have thrown the baby out with the bathwater. In rejecting the doctrines of Christianity that make Christ a vicarious sacrifice for our sins, we also seem to have forgotten that as flawed human beings we mess up at times, we don't always extend ourselves, and we don't always do the right thing. We are only human, and as such we going to miss the mark sometimes, whether through laziness, ignorance, flawed judgment, or an accident.

I often suggest that the Unitarian Universalist faith tradition could better meet the needs of humanity if it could admit there is a lot of suffering in the world and that much of it is of humanity's own making. Most have not had to overcome some great burden of guilt due to an intentional despicable act. However, what does

Unitarian Universalism really have to offer those who have screwed up in some way, have come to regret past transgressions, and now live with these burdens of guilt? Can Unitarian Universalism, as a faith tradition, claim any ritual, theology, or mythology that can lift that burden? There is much suffering in the world, and much of it is psychological and spiritual. Not all of it can be resolved through some social justice program. Guilt can happen to anyone at any time, even when we are basically good people who continually strive to lead upright lives.

Perhaps we could better serve a hurting world where so many feel burdened by guilt if we acknowledged that guilt and spoke to it ritually and liturgically. It is my prayer that my faith tradition might find a way to make it so for our community and for our world.

* * *

Postscript

Most everyone loves Jesus. Buddhists revere Jesus as a bodhisattva, many Hindus see Jesus as an avatar, and even Jews and Muslims see Jesus as a great wisdom teacher and a prophet. Some people love Jesus because of the Christian Church, and some love him in spite of it. In many interdenominational and interfaith social justice efforts of which I've been a part, the rallying cry became "Follow Jesus." The group recognized that even if we couldn't agree on basic points of theology or doctrine, we could find common ground and work together by emulating Jesus in his concern for the poor, the outcast, and the forgotten. Despite all our widely divergent opinions on points of doctrine and theology, Jesus seemed a good place to begin.

Progressive Christians often say that ours is the religion of Jesus rather than the religion about Jesus. That pithy statement makes a good point, but does that have any meaning beyond the implied emphasis on being like Jesus by living a life in service to others? Reading about the life of Jesus as recorded in the Gospels, the answer appears to be yes. He spent time ministering to a whole spectrum of human needs. However, the real thrust of his life was teaching twelve men how to live and relate to each other. Integral to this effort was the times he would retreat with the disciples and tell them stories about what he had seen and experienced with them. In many of those conversations, Jesus would reflect on Judaism, the religious tradition he shared with his disciples, and these reflections were an integral part of those small group conversations. The hypocrisy of the Pharisees, what the Sabbath is for, being in right relationship with one's neighbor before going to worship—these are just some of the inseparable parts of the religion of Jesus. He constantly initiated conversations about such issues. No religion of Jesus is complete without healthy reflection on the collective life and the traditions that inform spiritual practice. In that spirit was this book written. My reflections were committed to paper so as to be a part of a conversation. Thoughtful and constructive feedback is invited and appreciated.

This book has been about transforming faith. There is a deliberate double entendre in that phrase. "Transforming" can be used as an adjective to describe a particular kind of faith that leads a person to make changes in his or her life. It's faith that makes one more loving and open to life. I hope some of these stories will engender that type of faith in some of my readers.

"Transforming" can also be the progressive form of the verb "transform"—in this usage, the action of transforming or making changes to the faith of people's current understanding. I see this also as a part of the call as a people of faith. We are called to be change agents and to progressively transform current faith or the one handed down from the previous generation wherever it is deficient.

Times call for us to be together in new ways, revisit some of the old cherished ideas, make our faith relevant to the times in which we live, and lead where no one has yet dared to venture. We can't start these transformations. They're already underway. The question for us is whether we will be a part of it or be left behind. Will we look to the past or to the future? Those desperately caught up in preserving the ways of the past and reestablishing some golden age of the faith that probably never existed anyway damage the very tradition they are trying to preserve. The more they remain mired in the past, the more irrelevant their voices are to the conversation among those who want to make faith relevant to today's world and problems. We needn't be fearful of the future so long as we face it together united by a common Spirit.

Transforming faith happens in communities where honest and respectful conversations take place. Where we can know and be known. Where we can love and be loved. Let's begin.

Grace and Peace,
Fred

* * *

Acknowledgments

I wish to extend special thanks to Jan Livermore for reading an earlier version of the manuscript and making many helpful suggestions. The work would look quite different without her input. Also thanks to my wife and best friend, Kathy, for reading almost everything I write and for keeping me grounded in reality. Thanks to my congregation as well. You are my teacher every time I stand before you. Your attentiveness and encouragement gave me the self-confidence to attempt this book.

* * *

Selected Bibliography

Buber, Martin. *I and Thou*. New York: Touchstone, 1971.

Campbell, Joseph and Bill Moyers. *The Power of Myth*. New York: Doubleday, 1988.

Cousineau, Phil and Stuart Brown. *The Hero's Journey*. New York: Harper and Row, 1990.

Cox, Harvey. *The Future of Faith*. New York: Harper One, 2009.

Cox, Harvey. *The Seduction of the Spirit*. New York: Simon and Schuster, Inc., 1974.

Cox, Harvey. *When Jesus Came to Harvard*. New York: Houghton Mifflin Co., 2006.

Easwaran, Eknath. *Gandhi the Man*. Tomales: Nilgiri Press, 1997.

Fowler, James. *The Stages of Faith*. New York: Harper Collins, 1995.

Haidt, Jonathan. *The Happiness Hypothesis*. New York: Basic Books, 2006.

James, William. *The Varieties of Religious Experience*. (London: Longmans, Green & Co., 1902

Martel, Yann. *Life of Pi*. Orlando: Harcourt, Inc., 2001.

Palmer, Parker. *A Hidden Wholeness*. San Francisco: Jossey-Bass, 2004.

Peck, Scott. *Further Along the Road Less Traveled*. New York: Simon and Schuster, 1993.

Peck, Scott. *The Different Drum*. New York: Simon and Schuster, 1988.

Peck, Scott. *The Road Less Traveled*. New York: Touchstone, 1978.

Pollock, John. *The Apostle*. Wheaton: Victor Books, 1985.

Richardson, Robert. *The Mind on Fire*. Berkeley: University of California Press, 1995.

Russell, Bertrand. *The Autobiography of Bertrand Russell 1872-1914*. New York: Little, Brown and Co., 1967.

Thompson, Mel. *Philosophy of Religion*. London: Hodder Education, 2007.

Tillich, Paul. *Dynamics of Faith*. New York: Harper and Row, 1957.

Wood, Alan. *Bertrand Russell the Passionate Skeptic*. New York: Simon and Schuster, 1958.

* * *

Endnotes

Preface

A E. Wiesel, *The Gates of the Forest* (New York: Holt Rinehart and Winston, 1966), unnumbered pages preceding text.

B H. Cox, *The Seduction of the Spirit* (New York: Simon and Schuster, Inc., 1974), 9.

Introduction

C J. Goldstein and J. Kornfield, *Seeking the Heart of Wisdom* (Boston: Shambhala Publications, Inc., 1987), 105.

D M. Buber, *I and Thou*. Retrieved October 25, 2014, from http://www.tjdonovanart.com/Martin%20Buber%20-%20I%20And%20Thou%20%28c1923%20127P%29.pdf, 8-14.

Chapter 1

E J. Santino, The Fantasy and Folklore of All Hallows. *The American Folklife Center*, September 1982, Updated 2009. Retrieved September 23, 2014, from http://www.loc.gov/folklife/halloween.html.

Chapter 2

F J. Lennon, Imagine. *Imagine: Working Class Hero*, 1971 by Ascot Sound Studios Apple, LP.

G W. P. Howard and Y. Wozner, *Everyday Miracles: The Healing Wisdom of Hasidic Stories* (Northvale: Aronson, 1989), 47.

H D. Sheff, *All We Are Saying: The Last Major Interview with John Lennon and Yoko Ono*. ed. G. Barry Golson (New York: St Martin's Press, 1981), 212-213.

Chapter 3

I Y. Martel, *Life of Pi* (Orlando: Harcourt, Inc., 2001), ix.

J W. R. Greer, *HCSCENGLISH12*. Retrieved September 23, 2014, from http://hcscenglish12.wikispaces.com/%27Life+of+Pi%27+Reviews.

K D. Magee, Movie script, based on an original novel by Yann Martel. Retrieved September 23, 2014, from http://www.imsdb.com/scripts/Life-of-Pi.html.

L L. E. Turner, Review of the book and movie: *Life of Pi* by Yann Martel, January 17, 2013. Retrieved September 23, 2014, from http://loganeturner.com/2013/01/book-and-movie-review-life-of-pi-by-yann-martel.html.

M P. Viswanathan, Travels with My Tiger [Review of the book *Life of Pi*], fall and winter 2001–2002. Retrieved September 23, 2014, from http://aelaq.org/mrb-archives/feature.php?issue=6&article=59&cat=1.

N M. Thompson, *Philosophy of Religion* (London: Hodder Education, 2007), 114.

Chapter 5

O C. S. Lewis, Meditation in a Toolshed. *The Path to Light*. Retrieved September 24, 2014, from https://thepathtolight.com/uploads/C-S-Lewis-meditation-in-a-toolshed.pdf.

P J. Cutsinger, Paths of Return. *Cutsinger*. 2010, Retrieved October 28, 2014, from http://www.cutsinger.net/pdf/2010_paths_of_return.pdf.

Chapter 6

Q   J. Campbell and B. Moyers, *The Power of Myth*, ed. B. S. Flowers (New York: Doubleday, 1988), 196.

R   R. Richardson, *The Mind on Fire* (Berkeley: University of California Press, 1995), 227.

S   P. Cousineau and S. L. Brown, *The Hero's Journey* (New York: Harper and Row, 1990), vi.

T   S. Peck, *Further Along the Road Less Traveled* (New York: Simon and Schuster, 1993), 79.

Chapter 8

U   H. Cox, *The Future of Faith* (New York: Harper One, 2009), 3.

V   M. De Unamuno, St. Manuel, the Good, Martyr, trans. N. Mayberry, retrieved September 24, 2014, from http://www4.gvsu.edu/wrightd/SPA%20307%20Death/SaintManuelBueno.htm.

W   P. Tillich, *Dynamics of Faith* (New York: Harper and Row, 1957), 22.

X   S. Peck, *The Different Drum,* (New York: Simon and Schuster, 1988), 199-200.

Y   J. Fowler, *Stages of Faith* (New York: Harper Collins, 1995), 179.

Z   H. Cox, *The Future of Faith.* (New York: Harper One, 2009), 17.

Chapter 10

AA   J. Pollock, *The Apostle* (Wheaton: Victor Books, 1985), 34.

BB   J. Fowler, *Stages of Faith* (New York: Harper Collins, 1995), 164.

CC   S. Peck, The Stages of Spiritual Growth, retrieved October 27, 2014, from http://www.whale.to/b/peck1.html.

Chapter 11

DD   A. Seckel, *The Humanist Association of Los Angeles.* Retrieved October 27, 2014, from http://www.hala.org/quotes.html.

EE   A. Wood, *Bertrand Russell the Passionate Skeptic* (New York: Simon and Schuster, 1958), 21.
FF   L. Ahluwalia, *Understanding Philosophy of Religion*. (Oxford: OUP Oxford, 2008), 326–327.
GG   B. Russell, *The Autobiography of Bertrand Russell 1872–1914* (New York: Little, Brown and Co, 1967), 234–235.

Chapter 12
HH   A. Einstein, Gandhi (film), retrieved October 28, 2014, from http://en.wikiquote.org/wiki/Gandhi_%28film%29.
II   E. Easwaran, *Gandhi the Man* (Tomales: Nilgiri Press, 1997), 64.
JJ   Ibid.
KK   Ibid., 107.
LL   Ibid., 59.
MM   M. Gandhi, Gandhi (Film), retrieved October 28, 2014, from http://en.wikiquote.org/wiki/Gandhi_%28film%29.
NN   Ibid., 59.
OO   R. Wolsey, *Kissing Fish* (Bloomington: Xlibris Corporation, 2011), 268.
PP   J. Holmes and B. Southworth, *Mahatma Gandhi: An American Portrait* (Raleigh: Lulu.com, 2010) 22.
QQ   E. Easwaran, *Gandhi the Man* (Tomales: Nilgiri Press, 1997), 154.
RR   S. Ghose, *Mahatma Gandhi* (New Delhi: Allied Publishers, 1991), 378.

Chapter 13
SS   J. Taylor, My Stroke of Insight. Retrieved Oct 28, 2014, from http://blog.ted.com/2008/03/12/jill_bolte_tayl/#more.
TT   J. Taylor, My Stroke of Insight. *TED*, February 2008. Retrieved September 24, 2014, from http://blog.ted.com/2008/03/12/jill_bolte_tayl/#more.

UU W. James, *The Varieties of Religious Experience* (London: Longmans, Green & Co., 1902), 299–300.

VV H. Smith, *Cleansing the Doors of Perception* (Boulder: Sentient Publications, 2003), 26-27.

WW K. Armstrong, A Superhighway to Bliss. *The New York Times*, May 25, 2008. Retrieved September 24, 2014, from http://www.nytimes.com/2008/05/25/fashion/25brain.html?pagewanted=print&_r=0.

XX J. Taylor, My Stroke of Insight. Retrieved Oct 28, 2014, from http://blog.ted.com/2008/03/12/jill_bolte_tayl/#more.

Chapter 14
YY Documentary Hypothesis. *Wikipedia*. Retrieved September 24, 2014, from http://en.wikipedia.org/wiki/Documentary_hypothesis.

Chapter 16
ZZ L. Tolstoy, Two Old Men. *The Literature Network*, 1885. Retrieved September 24, 2014, from http://www.online-literature.com/tolstoy/2891/.

Chapter 17
AAA P. Palmer, *A Hidden Wholeness* (San Francisco: Jossey-Bass, 2004), 118–122.

Chapter 18
BBB S. Peck, *The Road Less Traveled* (New York: Touchstone, 1978), 81.

Chapter 19
CCC E. Abbott, Flatland, 1884. Retrieved September 24, 2014, from http://www.geom.uiuc.edu/~banchoff/Flatland/.

DDD   J. Haidt, *The Happiness Hypothesis* (New York: Basic Books, 2006), 182–184.
EEE   F. Vaughn, *Shadows of the Sacred* (Bloomington: iUniverse, 2005), 86.

Chapter 20
FFF   J. Osborne, One of Us. *Relish*, with Eric Bazilian and Rick Chertoff, 1995 by The Crawlspace. Compact disc.

Chapter 21
GGG   D. Mitchell, Why I Raise My Children Without God. *CNN iReport*, January 14, 2013. Retrieved September 24, 2014, from http://ireport.cnn.com/docs/DOC-910282.
HHH   Ibid.
III   S. Peck, *The Road Less Traveled* (New York: Touchstone, 1978), 197.
JJJ   Ibid., 197–221.
KKK   Ibid., 223.
LLL   D. Sashin, Godless Mom strikes a Chord with Parents. *CNN belief Blog*. Retrieved October 31, 2014, from http://religion.blogs.cnn.com/2013/01/18/godless-mom-strikes-a-chord-with-parents/.

Chapter 22
MMM   J. Campbell and B. Moyers, *The Power of Myth*, ed. B. S. Flowers (New York: Doubleday, 1988), 49.
NNN   H. Schleifer, TEDxTelAviv–Hedy Schleifer– The Power of Connection. Retrieved October 31, 2014, from http://www.allreadable.com/82035SD.

Chapter 23
OOO   D. E. Parkerson, *Bloom Where You Are Planted. Martin Buber's Tales of the Hasidim*, February 11, 2011. Retrieved September 24, 2014, from http://www.brnow.org/Opinions/

Opinion-Archives/The-Paper-Pulpit/February-2011/
Bloom-Where-You-Are-Planted.

PPP   J. Campbell and B. Moyers, *The Power of Myth*, ed. B. S.
Flowers (New York: Doubleday, 1988), 218-219.

Chapter 26

QQQ   H. Cox, *When Jesus Came to Harvard* (New York: Houghton
Mifflin Co., 2006), 274.

RRR   P. Rollins, My Confession: I Deny the Resurrection. *Peter
Rollins*, January 1, 2009. Retrieved September 25, 2014, from http://
peterrollins.net/2009/01/my-confession-i-deny-the-resurrection/.

Chapter 27

SSS   Zen. *Spiritual Minds*. Retrieved September 25, 2014, from
http://spiritual-minds.com/stories/zen.htm.

TTT   E. Whitehead and J. Whitehead, *Transforming Our Painful
Emotions* (New York: Orbis Books, 2010), 93.

UUU   S. Peck, *Further Along the Road Less Traveled* (New York:
Simon and Schuster, 1993), 158–159.

* * *

Author Biography

Born and raised in Macon, Georgia, Fred Howard is an ordained minister by the Christian Universalist Association and is currently the minister of the Unitarian Church of Valdosta, Georgia. He graduated in 2006 from Candler School of Theology at Emory in Atlanta and spent a year in the Clinical Pastoral Education program at Emory Hospital. Prior to that, he attended Valdosta State College and the Medical College of Georgia, and practiced medicine for twenty years.

Active in his church and community, Howard is married to Kathy Riggins Howard and lives in Valdosta. They have three grown children, Mandy, Misty, and Dustin, and six grandchildren.

* * *

Made in the USA
Lexington, KY
10 December 2014